WHY READ AND STUDY THE BOOK OF MARK?

The kingdom of God is breaking into our world. It first arrived with the coming of Jesus, and ever since it has been spreading over the whole earth, offering a new way of life to people everywhere. The very fact that you're holding this book in your hands means that it has reached you. But how will you respond to the kingdom?

Becoming part of the kingdom can be a scary thought. It means giving up everything to follow Jesus. It could cost you your friends, your money, your career. There are no guarantees of comfort or safety. You will not be in control.

At the same time, becoming part of the kingdom is the most exciting thought you'll ever entertain. It will make you part of a community built on values of love, service, generosity, humility and hope. It will give you the opportunity to find healing and deliverance, and to share these things with others as well. It will send you on adventures you couldn't have imagined. People from all over the world will become your brothers and sisters in the faith. And best of all, you'll meet Jesus and get to know him better each day.

So which will it be? Will you catch the wave as the kingdom rolls by? Or will you decide it's just too unpredictable to stake your life on? The choice can be difficult.

That's why the Bible contains a book by a man named Mark that was written for people facing this very decision. They lived in a time and place—the city of Rome during the reign of Nero—when following Jesus could literally cost them their lives. Mark retells the story of Jesus' life for them in a brisk, vigorous narrative that flows like a stage drama. He steadily reveals who Jesus is and shows different characters either embracing the kingdom with bold faith or stepping back to let it pass by. The book ends with a challenge: Which characters will you be like?

Mark is a master storyteller, so his book is a delight to read. It's even better when you read it aloud in a group and talk about it together. That's what this guide will help you do. So get together with some friends and let Mark introduce you to Jesus and invite you to become part of the kingdom of God. You'll never face a more important question. And there's no better way to consider it than by hearing the story of Jesus.

UNDERSTANDING THE
BOOKS OF THE BIBLE

MARK

Also available in the Understanding the Books of the Bible series:

John
Genesis
Wisdom: Proverbs/Ecclesiastes/James
Biblical Apocalypses: Daniel/Revelation
Paul's Journey Letters: Thessalonians/Corinthians/
    Galatians/Romans
Lyric Poetry: Psalms/Song of Songs/Lamentations
Paul's Prison Letters: Colossians/Ephesians/Philemon/
    Philippians/Timothy/Titus
New Covenants: Deuteronomy/Hebrews
Isaiah
Joshua/Judges/Ruth
Luke-Acts
Job

Future releases:

Prophets Before the Exile: Amos/Hosea/Micah/Zephaniah/
    Nahum/Habakkuk

UNDERSTANDING THE BOOKS OF THE BIBLE

MARK

Christopher R. Smith

An imprint of InterVarsity Press
Downers Grove, Illinois

InterVarsity Press
P.O. Box 1400, Downers Grove, IL 60515-1426
World Wide Web: www.ivpress.com
E-mail: email@ivpress.com

©2013 by Christopher R. Smith

All rights reserved. No part of this book may be reproduced in any form without written permission from InterVarsity Press.

InterVarsity Press® is the book-publishing division of InterVarsity Christian Fellowship/USA®, a movement of students and faculty active on campus at hundreds of universities, colleges and schools of nursing in the United States of America, and a member movement of the International Fellowship of Evangelical Students. For information about local and regional activities, write Public Relations Dept., InterVarsity Christian Fellowship/USA, 6400 Schroeder Rd., P.O. Box 7895, Madison, WI 53707-7895, or visit the IVCF website at <www.intervarsity.org>.

All Scripture quotations, unless otherwise indicated, are taken from THE HOLY BIBLE, NEW INTERNATIONAL VERSION®, NIV® *Copyright © 1973, 1978, 1984, 2011 by Biblica, Inc.™ Used by permission. All rights reserved worldwide.*

Design: Cindy Kiple
Images: © Stanislav Pobytov/iStockphoto

ISBN 978-0-8308-5813-2

Printed in the United States of America ∞

InterVarsity Press is committed to protecting the environment and to the responsible use of natural resources. As a member of Green Press Initiative we use recycled paper whenever possible. To learn more about the Green Press Initiative, visit <www.greenpressinitiative.org>.

P	20	19	18	17	16	15	14	13	12	11	10	9	8	7	6	5	4	3	2	1
Y	30	29	28	27	26	25	24	23	22	21	20	19	18	17	16	15	14	13		

CONTENTS

Why Read and Study the Book of Mark?	i
How These Study Guides Are Different	1
Outline of Mark	10
Map of Locations Mentioned in Mark	11

SESSION 1
Experiencing the Gospel of Mark as a Whole — 13

SESSION 2
Mark Introduces Jesus as the Messiah and the Son of God — 17

SESSION 3
Jesus Proclaims God's Coming Kingdom by
Teaching, Healing, and Delivering — 22

SESSION 4
The Religious Leaders Challenge Jesus' Teachings and Activities — 27

SESSION 5
Jesus Appoints Twelve Disciples, and His Family Joins the Opposition — 32

SESSION 6
Jesus Tells Parables About His Message,
His Identity, and the Kingdom of God — 37

SESSION 7
Jesus Calms a Storm and Drives Out a Legion of Demons — 42

SESSION 8
Jesus Does Two More Great Miracles, but
He's Rejected in His Hometown — 46

SESSION 9
Jesus Sends His Disciples Out, and
Mark Reports the Fate of John the Baptist — 50

SESSION 10
Jesus Feeds Five Thousand People and Walks on the Water — 54

SESSION 11
Jesus Declares All Foods Clean and Ministers Among the Gentiles — 58

SESSION 12
The Identity of Jesus Comes into Focus
Through a Repeated Series of Events — 63

SESSION 13
Jesus Predicts His Sufferings and Appears in Glory on a Mountaintop — 68

SESSION 14
    Jesus Delivers a Boy from a Demon and Teaches His Disciples Privately   73

SESSION 15
    Jesus Teaches His Disciples More About the
    Ways of the Kingdom of God   78

SESSION 16
    Jesus Teaches About Greatness and Heals Blind Bartimaeus   82

SESSION 17
    Jesus Enters Jerusalem, Makes a Fig Tree Wither,
    and Cleanses the Temple   86

SESSION 18
    The Jewish Leaders Question Jesus' Authority and Identity   90

SESSION 19
    Jesus Debates His Opponents and Teaches the Crowds in the Temple   94

SESSION 20
    Jesus Predicts the Destruction of the Temple   99

SESSION 21
    Jesus Shares a Meal in Bethany and Observes Passover in Jerusalem   104

SESSION 22
    Jesus Prays in Gethsemane and Is Arrested and
    Questioned by the Sanhedrin   108

SESSION 23
    Jesus Gives His Life as the Savior of the World   112

SESSION 24
    Jesus Is Buried and Rises from the Dead   116

HOW THESE STUDY GUIDES ARE DIFFERENT

Did you know you could read and study the Bible without using any chapters or verses? The books of the Bible are real "books." They're meant to be experienced the same way other books are: as exciting, interesting works that keep you turning pages right to the end and then make you want to go back and savor each part. The UNDERSTANDING THE BOOKS OF THE BIBLE series of study guides will help you do that with the Bible.

While you can use these guides with any version or translation, they're especially designed to be used with *The Books of the Bible*, an edition of the Scriptures from Biblica that takes out the chapter and verse numbers and presents the biblical books in their natural form. Here's what people are saying about reading the Bible this way:

> I love it. I find myself understanding Scripture in a new way, with a fresh lens, and I feel spiritually refreshed as a result. I learn much more through stories being told and, with this new format, I feel the truth of the story come alive for me.

> Reading Scripture this way flows beautifully. I don't miss the chapter and verse numbers. I like them gone. They got in the way.

> I've been a reader of the Bible all of my life. But after reading just a few pages without chapters and verses, I was amazed at what I'd been missing all these years.

For more information about *The Books of the Bible* or to obtain a copy of this specially designed edition, visit www.biblica.com/thebooks. Watch the site for a four-volume set comprising the entire Bible in this format, now in progress. A trade edition of the full Bible is also available from Zondervan, online or through your favorite Christian book retailer.

For people who are used to chapters and verses, reading and studying the Bible without them may take a little getting used to. It's like when you get a new smart phone, or move from using a laptop to a tablet. You have to unlearn some old ways of doing things and learn some new ways. But it's not too long until you catch on to how the new system works and you find you can do a lot of things you couldn't do before.

Here are some of the ways you and your group will have a better experience of the Scriptures by using these study guides.

YOU'LL FOLLOW THE NATURAL FLOW OF BIBLICAL BOOKS

This guide will take you through the book of Mark following its natural flow. (The way this book unfolds is illustrated in the outline on page 10.) You won't go chapter-by-chapter, because chapter divisions in the Bible often come at the wrong places and break up the flow. Did you know that the chapters found in most modern Bibles were added more than a thousand years after the biblical books were written? And that the verse numbers were added more than three centuries after that? If you grew up with the chapter-and-verse system, it may feel like part of the inspired Word of God. But it's not. Those little numbers aren't holy, and when you read and study the Bible without them, you'll hear its message more clearly than ever before.

To help you get a feel for where you are in each book's natural flow, the sessions will be headed by a visual cue, like this:

Gospel of Mark > Part One: Who is Jesus? > Act 1: Jesus and the Religious Teachers

YOU'LL UNDERSTAND WHOLE BOOKS

Imagine going to a friend's house to watch a movie you've never seen before. After only a couple of scenes, your friend stops the film and says, "So, tell me what you think of it so far." When you give your best shot at a reply, based on the little you've seen, your friend says, "You know, there's a scene in another movie that always makes me think of this one." He switches to a different movie and before you know it, you're watching a scene from the middle of another film.

Who would ever try to watch a movie this way? Yet many study guides take this approach to the Bible. They have you read a few paragraphs from one book, then jump to a passage in another book. The UNDERSTANDING THE BOOKS OF THE BIBLE series doesn't do that. Instead, these study guides focus on understanding the message and meaning of one book at a time. Your group will read through Mark in its entirety, not just selected chapters or verses. In order to accomplish this, the readings for each session will be a little longer than the ones you may be used to doing in Bible study groups. However, they'll still take only about 5–10 minutes on average, and they'll give you a comprehensive understanding of the books you're considering. Your group should take a moment after each reading to allow people to ask about any words or phrases that weren't clear so you can work to understand these together.

Session 1 is an overview that will let you experience the book of Mark as a whole, to prepare you for considering its individual sections. *You should arrange for a little extra meeting time for this session.* Reading through an entire book at once will be like viewing a whole movie before zooming in on one scene. Groups that read books of the Bible aloud together have a great experience doing this. (If you've never done it before, give it a try—you'll be surprised at how well it flows and how fast the time passes.)

Alternatively, you can listen to a professional recording of the book (although we really recommend reading it aloud together in your group). If you do, you should listen to it in the latest update to the New International Version (NIV), since that's the translation used in *The Books of the Bible* and in these studies. You can, for example, listen to the book over the Internet at www.biblegateway.com/resources/audio.

For this overview session the discussion will be briefer and designed to allow people to share their overall impressions. If you're using *The Books of the Bible*, you may find it helpful to read the introduction to Mark in that edition out loud together before reading the book itself.

YOU'LL DECIDE FOR YOURSELVES WHAT TO DISCUSS

In each session of this study guide there are many options for discussion. While each session could be completed by a group in about an hour and a half, any one of the questions could lead to an involved conversation. There's no need to cut the conversation short to try to "get through it all." Group leaders can read through all the questions ahead of time and decide which one(s) to begin with, and in what order to take them up. Make any preparations necessary for the questions you choose. (For example, you may need to ensure that the group has Internet access.) If you do get into an involved discussion of one question, you can leave out some of the others, or you can extend the study over more than one meeting if you do want to cover them all.

TOGETHER, YOU'LL TELL THE STORY

The book of Mark tells the story of Jesus, which is the culmination of the story of God that unfolds throughout the Bible, in order to help its original audience recognize where they fit within that larger story. As you retell the story of Jesus out loud in your group, you'll discover where you fit as well.

Each session offers suggestions for how the reading can be done creatively and meaningfully. The guide will often invite the group to dramatize the Scriptures by reading them out loud like a play. The discussion options may invite group members to retell the biblical story from fresh perspectives—for example, from the point of view of one of the characters, or of a person today who's in a similar situation. This kind of telling and retelling is a spiritual discipline, similar to Bible memorization, that allows people to personalize the Scriptures and take them to heart. This discipline is very timely in a culture that increasingly appreciates the value and authority of story.

If you're using *The Books of the Bible* (and you'll have the best experience of this guide with that edition), you'll find that the natural sections it marks off with white space match up with the sections of the reading. But even if you are using another edition of the Bible, you'll be able to identify these sections easily because their openings and closings will be clearly described.

EVERYBODY WILL PARTICIPATE

There's plenty of opportunity for everyone to participate, by reading the Scriptures or by introducing the study or the discussion questions to the group. Group leaders can involve quiet people naturally by giving them these opportunities. And everyone will feel they can respond, because the questions aren't looking for "right answers." Instead, they invite people to reflect on deeper issues and pursue an understanding of them together, even if everybody doesn't agree in the end.

YOU'LL ALL SHARE DEEPLY

The discussion questions will invite you to share deeply about your ideas and experiences. The answers to these questions can't be found just by "looking them up." They require reflection on the meaning of each passage, in the wider context of the book it belongs to, in light of your personal experience. These aren't the kinds of abstract, academic questions that make the discussion feel like a test. Instead, they'll connect the Bible passage to your life in practical, personal, relational ways.

To create a climate of trust where this kind of deep sharing is encouraged, here are a couple of ground rules that your group should agree to at its first meeting:

Confidentiality. Group members agree to keep what is shared in the group strictly confidential. "What's said in the group stays in the group."

Respect. Group members will treat other members with respect at all times, even when disagreeing over ideas.

HOW TO LEAD GROUP STUDIES USING THIS GUIDE

Each session has three basic parts:

Introduction to the Study

Have a member of your group read the introduction to the session out loud to everyone. (If it's a longer introduction, group members can take turns reading a paragraph each.) Then give everyone the chance to ask questions about the introduction, and offer their own thoughts and examples.

Reading from Mark

Read the selection out loud together. The study guide will offer suggestions for various ways you can do this for each session. (In some sessions, reading and discussion will be combined.) Give people a chance to ask about words, phrases, or concepts they didn't understand in the reading.

Discussion Questions

Most questions are introduced with some observations. These may give some background to the history and culture of the ancient world, or explain where you are in the flow of the book. After these observations there are suggested discussion questions. Many of them have multiple parts that are really just different ways of getting at an issue.

You don't have to discuss the questions in the order they appear in the study guide. You can choose to spend your time exploring just one or two questions, and not do the others. Or you can have shorter discussion of each question so that you do cover all of them. Before the meeting group leaders should read through the questions and the observations that introduce them, and decide which ones they want to emphasize.

When you get to a given question, have someone read aloud the observations and the question. As you answer the question, interact with the observations (you can agree or disagree with them) in light of your reading from the Bible. Use only part of the question to get at the issue from one angle, or use all of the parts, as you choose. (Occasionally questions will be asked as part of the introduction to the study.)

TIPS FOR HOME GROUPS, SUNDAY SCHOOL CLASSES, COMMUNITY BIBLE EXPERIENCES AND INDIVIDUAL USE

If you're using this guide in a *home group*, you may want to begin each meeting (or at least some meetings) by having dinner together. You may also want to have a time of singing and prayer before or after the study.

If you're using this guide in a *Sunday school class*, you may want to have a time of singing and prayer before or after the study.

This study guide can also be used in connection with a *community Bible experience*. If you're using it in this way in your church:

- Encourage people to read each session's Scripture passage by themselves early in the week (except for session 1, when the whole community should gather together to hear Mark read out loud).
- Do each session in midweek small groups.
- Invite people to write/create some response to each small-group session that could be shared in worship that weekend. These might involve poetry, journal or blog entries, artwork, dramas, videos and so on. Some of these may be created because of specific questions in this guide that invite and encourage artistic responses.
- During the weekend worship services, let people share these responses, and have preaching on the topic of the session that was done that week. Speakers can gather up comments they've heard from people and draw on their own reflections to sum up the church's experience of that session.
- During the following week the community will then read, discuss and respond to the Scriptures for the next session, and the worship gathering will once more center around these responses.

This guide can also be used for *individual study*. You can write out your responses to the questions in a notebook or journal. (However, we really encourage reading and studying the Bible in community!)

MARK

OUTLINE OF THE GOSPEL OF MARK
(numbers in parentheses indicate sessions in this guide)

PROLOGUE (1)
- Identifies Jesus as the Messiah and the Son of God

PART ONE: WHO IS JESUS?
Depicts Jesus teaching, healing, and delivering in Galilee.
This raises the question of his identity.

Act I: Jesus and the Religious Teachers (2-4)
- Begins with a scene of Jesus engaging his disciples
  Jesus calls Peter, Andrew, James, and John to follow him.
- Ends with the religious teachers reaching a conclusion about Jesus

Act II: Jesus and His Family and Neighbors (5-8)
- Begins with a scene of Jesus engaging his disciples
  Jesus chooses twelve disciples to "be with him" and observe his work closely.
- Presents a concentrated block of Jesus' teaching
  Parables about the kingdom of God
- Ends with Jesus' family and neighbors reaching a conclusion about him

Act III: Jesus and His Disciples (9-12)
- Begins with a scene of Jesus engaging his disciples
  Jesus sends the disciples out on their own to teach, heal, and deliver.
- In the next-to-last episode, the healing of a blind man in stages symbolizes the disciples slowly coming to understand
- Ends with the disciples reaching a conclusion about Jesus

PART TWO: WHO JESUS IS
Jesus' identity is clarified as he travels to Jerusalem,
teaches his disciples, confronts the religious establishment,
and gives his life as the Savior of the world.

Act IV: Journey to Jerusalem (13-16)
- In the last episode, the healing of a blind man all at once symbolizes the disciples seeing Jesus much more clearly

Act V: Confrontation in Jerusalem (17-20)
- Presents a concentrated block of Jesus' teaching
  Jesus predicts the destruction of the temple.

Act VI: Jesus' Sufferings, Death, and Resurrection (21-24)

LOCATIONS MENTIONED IN THE GOSPEL OF MARK

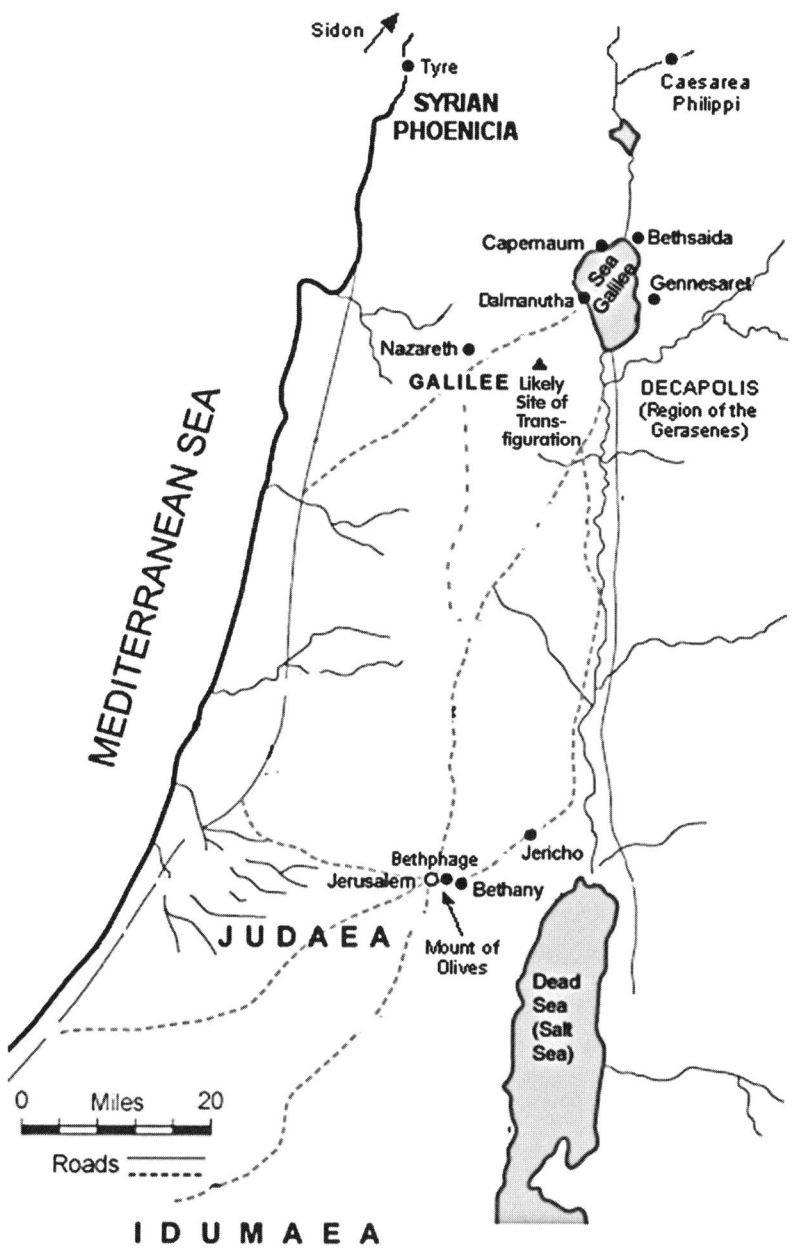

SESSION 1

EXPERIENCING THE GOSPEL OF MARK AS A WHOLE

INTRODUCTION

Four different books in the New Testament tell the story of Jesus: Mark, Matthew, John and Luke (the first part of Luke-Acts). These books were all written about a generation after Jesus lived. Each one selects and arranges materials passed down from his time to communicate a particular message about who Jesus is and what it means to follow him. In this guide we'll be exploring one of these books—Mark.

The author of this book doesn't identify himself by name. He doesn't say where or when he's writing, or who he's writing for. But much information about this can be inferred from the book itself. The way the author often uses Latin terms instead of Greek ones suggests that he's writing for a Roman audience. The way he explains Jewish customs and translates Aramaic phrases suggests that this audience is living some distance from the land of Palestine and isn't familiar with the language and culture there. Taken together, all of the indications in the book provide good support for the belief that it was composed by a particular historical figure whose name actually was Mark. He was a friend and companion of the apostle Peter, who was one of the people who got to know Jesus the best.

Shortly before or after Peter's execution in Rome by the emperor Nero in AD 65, Mark drew on the recollections Peter had shared with him, along with information that others had passed down, to craft an artful retelling of the story of Jesus. He did this to communicate to the remaining believers in Rome how vital it was for them to remain loyal to Jesus, no matter what the cost.

Several leaders of the community of Jesus' followers who lived in the next few centuries offer precisely this account of the book's origins. While it has been debated in more recent centuries, this view is still widely respected among biblical scholars today, and it is the one that will be followed in this study guide. (More of the grounds for this understanding is presented in the introduction to Mark in *The Books of the Bible*, which your group may want to look at together before reading the book itself.)

As Mark introduces his story about Jesus, he calls it "the good news." This is how Jesus' earliest followers most often described the story of his life, death and resurrection. The expression "good news" is the source of the English word *gospel*. Mark's book, like the others in the Bible that tell the story of Jesus, is often described as a gospel, and that is how we will refer to it here.

READING

In this session you'll read through the whole gospel of Mark. This should take about an hour. It will help you situate individual passages within the overall flow of the book. If you're using *The Books of the Bible*, you can find Mark in the Table of Contents. If you're using another version, Mark will likely be the second book in the New Testament.

Have members of your group who are good at reading aloud and who enjoy doing so take turns reading through the book, switching whenever they come to what feels like a natural break. (Note: Most scholars agree that the book originally ended with the line "They said nothing to anyone, because they were afraid." The material that follows in most Bibles, which is italicized in the NIV, was likely added later to give the book a more satisfying ending. Read all the way through to the end of this material, which represents the traditional conclusion of the book. You'll have the chance to discuss how Mark ends when you do the final session in this guide.)

As you're listening, you can find the cities and regions mentioned in the book on the map on page 11. You can follow how the book develops by looking at the outline on page 10. There Mark is described as like a drama or play that's presented in six acts. Biblical scholars widely consider the book to share many of the characteristics of the dramas that were staged in Roman times. In the sessions ahead you'll read much of the book out loud in parts like a play, to bring out this dramatic character.

Mark is admired as an excellent storyteller. You'll notice how the action moves swiftly from one scene to another, as Mark ties episodes together with phrases like "at once," "just then" and "immediately." Note as well the places where Mark starts one story and then switches to another before telling how the first one turned out, creating suspense that draws his listeners in. Many interpreters believe that the book was meant to be read out loud to its audience. It has many of the characteristics of oral literature, including devices that allow the listeners to catch up with what they've been hearing, such as summaries of the action and doubled expressions (for example, "casting a net into the lake, for they were fishermen"; "very early in the morning, while it was still dark"). One scholar of the book has noted, "Mark was designed for oral transmission—and for transmission as a continuous whole—rather than for private study or silent reading."[1] In this session you'll have the opportunity to experience it the way its author intended.

The main theme of Mark is the identity of Jesus. The first half of the book poses the question, "Who is Jesus?" It shows the religious teachers of the time, his family and neighbors, and his disciples all wrestling with this question. The second half of the book steadily reveals more about who Jesus is as he travels to Jerusalem, teaches the people there, and finally gives his life on the cross and is raised from the dead. But the book then ends abruptly, challenging its original listeners, and all who've heard it since, to follow Jesus boldly and openly, in order to complete in their own lives this story that Mark provocatively leaves unfinished in the pages of the Bible.

---

[1]Christopher Bryan, *A Preface to Mark* (Oxford: Oxford University Press, 1993), 152.

DISCUSSION

◐ Was this the first time you'd ever read a whole book of the Bible out loud in a group? If so, what was the experience like for you? How did it compare with other ways you may have read the Bible before, either alone or with other people? If you have read other biblical books out loud in a group before, describe those experiences and share how this one compared with them.

◐ What things in the gospel of Mark struck you the most as you listened? What were your favorite parts of the book? Were there things that you didn't like, or that didn't make sense to you? (Make a note of them now, and be sure to bring them up when you get to that part of the book in the sessions ahead.)

◐ What did you learn about Jesus from listening to the whole gospel of Mark?

◐ The following story was recently told on a blog. A young man who thought of the Bible only as a "weird book you found in hotel rooms" had the opportunity to read through the gospel of Mark out loud on a road trip with a friend. By the time they were done, he said he wanted to read the rest of the Bible, too. Why do you think the experience had this effect on him?

… SESSION 2

MARK INTRODUCES JESUS AS THE MESSIAH AND THE SON OF GOD

Gospel of Mark > Prologue

INTRODUCTION

Mark begins with a prologue that's distinct from the main narrative of the book in several ways. It takes place out in the wilderness, in the barren, rocky Jordan River basin, rather than in the world of human culture and society. From the wilderness it gives us a glimpse into the spiritual realm that will be largely hidden behind the human world in the rest of the book. It explains how events fulfill scriptural prophecies, and it identifies the spiritual forces and personalities that will be active behind the scenes in subsequent episodes. Most importantly, the prologue to Mark answers the question that the characters in the narrative will be wrestling with: "Who is Jesus?"

Mark announces that Jesus is the Messiah, the deliverer God promised to send the people of Israel, and the Son of God, the divine agent of human salvation. The key characters in the prologue know that Jesus is these things, and they reveal this to the book's audience. As a result, the audience will experience the main narrative knowing something its characters don't. This effect (known as "dramatic irony") is designed to lead the audience to respond with insight and urgency once they've heard the whole story that Mark tells about Jesus.

READING

Have three members of your group read the three episodes in Mark's prologue, starting at these places:
- "The beginning of the good news about Jesus"
- "At that time Jesus came from Nazareth"
- "At once the Spirit sent him out into the wilderness" (ending with "angels attended him")

DISCUSSION

1 God sent a man named John to prepare the people of Israel for the coming of Jesus. Mark says this fulfilled God's promises as recorded in the Scriptures. Although he names only the prophet Isaiah, he actually quotes from the books of Exodus ("I will send my messenger ahead of you") and Malachi (the messenger will "prepare the way") before citing Isaiah's prophecy that a "voice calling in the wilderness" would help get the Israelites ready for the Messiah.

John delivers his message in a way that underscores its urgency. By leaving human society, by eating food that requires no cultivation, and by wearing only primitive clothing, he dramatizes that preparing for the Messiah is so important that people should drop everything, even pursuits basic to human survival, to get right with God. John tells the huge crowds that to be forgiven of the wrong things they've done, they need to repent—stop doing these things—and be baptized. The people respond by confessing (admitting) what they'd done wrong and by having John baptize them.

Baptism meant being washed entirely in water as a sign of a new beginning.[1] This ceremony, too, emphasized the urgency of John's message. It was used at this time to bring Gentile converts into the Jewish faith, and so here it insisted that each of John's listeners, even though they were already Jews, had to make a fresh start with God on the basis of repentance and forgiveness.

---

[1] Because John performed this ceremony, he became known as "the Baptizer." This is usually translated "the Baptist" in English, as in the NIV. However, John was not a Baptist in the sense of the word today. Historically, Baptist churches had their beginnings in the seventeenth century.

John then explains that even this is only a beginning. He has actually come to announce that another, more powerful figure will follow right after him. Repentance, confession and forgiveness are not ends in themselves; they're designed to bring people to the place where they will be ready to respond to this figure. John says that the coming Messiah will baptize the people with the Holy Spirit. The Greek verb "baptize" means to fill by immersing. It describes, for example, filling a cup by plunging it in a jar of water, or coloring cloth by dipping it in dye. (Mark will use the term in this sense later in the gospel to describe the washing of cups and pitchers.) The implication of its use here is that those who respond to Jesus will be filled and surrounded by the Spirit as they begin a new life.

> What do you think it would have been like to be part of a giant crowd going out into an uninhabited area to hear a speaker like John? What's the closest thing to this you've ever experienced?

> John explains that baptism is supposed to constitute the beginning of a new life. It's not supposed to be just a ceremony that's only meaningful at the time. What makes a baptism "stick"? That is, what enables a person to live out the meaning of their baptism for the rest of their life? Find out which people in your group have been baptized for the longest time and ask them to share their reflections on this question.

> It's often said that a person becomes a genuine follower of Jesus by confessing and repenting of their sins and receiving forgiveness from God. But John the Baptist suggests that this is actually only a prelude to following Jesus, and that an actual encounter with him will be a dynamic spiritual transaction that fills and empowers a person with the Holy Spirit. Where would you put yourself on the spectrum that's illustrated here in the prologue to Mark?

> **a.** On the outside looking in, like a Gentile of the time considering conversion to Judaism
> **b.** Raised in a religious setting, like the Jews who came to hear John

c. Forgiven by God after confessing and repenting of sin
d. Filled and empowered by the Holy Spirit after dynamically encountering Jesus

What are the next practical steps you'd like to take to move along the spectrum into a deeper experience of faith in Jesus?

2 Mark's opening Scripture quotations and John's prediction of the powerful figure to come identify Jesus as the Messiah. At his baptism, Jesus is then identified as the Son of God. Jesus was baptized not because he had to repent of sin, but because he wanted to identify publicly with the movement of God that John was announcing. Mark focuses on how Jesus saw a vision of heaven opened and heard a voice speak from above. He does this to emphasize how this moment confirmed Jesus' own sense of identity. Mark's audience is allowed to share the experience, but the characters in the book will have to engage Jesus in a variety of circumstances before reaching their own conclusions about him.

> ⊃ The voice from heaven assures Jesus of his unique identity as a divine agent of salvation. But its words, taken another way, apply to anyone who is restored to relationship with God through faith in Jesus. Have you ever felt God assuring you that you are his own son or daughter and that he loves you and is well pleased with you? If so, share your experience with the group. If not, what would it mean to you to hear God telling you this?

3 The Spirit sends Jesus to spend forty days out in the wilderness. Mark relates this episode much more briefly than other gospel writers. His terse account mirrors the sparse conditions in which the trappings of civilization are stripped away and the spiritual conflict that will surround Jesus' future mission becomes apparent. On one side Jesus is threatened by Satan and dangerous wild animals; on the other side he's helped by the guiding Spirit and attending angels. (Many commentators believe that the animals, which aren't in the longer accounts in Matthew and Luke, are mentioned here as an allusion to the wild animals that loyal followers of Jesus faced in Roman stadiums.) This wilderness experience shows Jesus the struggle that lies ahead but also assures him of God's presence and help.

➲ Many followers of Jesus go through a "wilderness experience" at some point in their lives. Without actually leaving civilization, they find themselves outside their accustomed role and position, tested and threatened in a situation where they have no status or security, but also cared for and guided intimately by God. Such an experience helps people see the spiritual dimensions of their lives in sharper focus. It is often a prelude to a season of greater influence and effectiveness. If you or someone you know has gone through an experience like this, describe it for the group. What would you, or the person who went through it, say was the value of this experience?

SESSION 3

JESUS PROCLAIMS GOD'S COMING KINGDOM BY TEACHING, HEALING, AND DELIVERING

Gospel of Mark > Part One > Act I: Jesus and the Religious Teachers

INTRODUCTION

The first part of the gospel of Mark raises the question "Who is Jesus?" In three acts, it shows different groups of people wrestling with this question. Act I depicts how the religious teachers were confronted with the message of Jesus and how they ultimately decided to resist it. The opening scenes of this act portray the powerful and liberating character of Jesus' ministry itself, before this conflict becomes overt.

READING

Read the opening episodes of Act I, beginning with "After John was put in prison" and ending with "Yet the people still came to him from everywhere." Read these episodes out loud like a play. (You can leave out cues like "Jesus said," "Jesus replied," etc.) Have people take these parts:
- Narrator
- Jesus
- Man in the synagogue possessed by a spirit

- People in the synagogue
- Simon
- Man with leprosy

(The narrator has the longest part; you may wish to have two people share this role, with the second narrator taking over after the scene in the synagogue. Also, have one spokesperson represent all the people in the synagogue and speak their lines. Do this whenever there's a group part in the readings.)

DISCUSSION

1 Act I begins with a scene of Jesus engaging his disciples. Acts II and III begin the same way. In this case he calls his first four disciples, who leave their homes and livelihoods to follow him.

➲ What do you think motivated Simon, Andrew, James, and John to abandon their previous lives in order to travel with Jesus as his disciples? Was this an extraordinary act, expected only of the first apostles, or are all followers of Jesus expected to do something like this?

2 Jesus' mission is to proclaim that the kingdom of God is arriving. He does this through his teaching and his acts of healing and exorcism. Mark summarizes Jesus' proclamation about the kingdom here, but he doesn't define or explain what this kingdom is. Instead, he'll get readers to explore its meaning throughout the course of his gospel.

Mark also doesn't divulge the content of Jesus' teaching in these early episodes. Readers will soon learn about his teachings as he corrects the religious teachers' misconceptions. But we do discover here that Jesus teaches with "authority, not as the teachers of the law." Those teachers would catalog various people's opinions about questions relating to the law God gave to Israel through Moses and present audiences with an array of options without really resolving a matter. By contrast, Jesus (as we'll soon see) gave incisive and convincing answers that reflected a broad grasp and profound understanding of the Scriptures. As a result, "The people were amazed at his teaching."

◌ Even people who don't have a religious faith in Jesus consider him to be one of the greatest teachers who ever lived. What makes his teaching, as you understand it, so distinctive and influential?

3 The people are even more amazed by Jesus' acts of healing and exorcism. By raising up a woman who's bedridden with a dangerous fever, by cleansing a leper and by driving out demons, Jesus shows that through his ministry, God's coming kingdom is liberating people from the affliction of disease and the bondage of spiritual oppression.

◌ Mark says that Jesus healed "many," but not "all," of the people who gathered around Simon's house. Jesus didn't come to make a complete end of all disease, but rather to announce the coming of God's kingdom through acts of mercy and liberation. Many followers of Jesus believe that these declarative acts continue to this day. If you feel that you or someone you know has received a divine healing in Jesus' name, tell your group about it.

◌ In the exorcisms described here, Jesus delivers people who have come under the controlling influence of supernatural beings that are hostile to God. Mark refers to these beings as demons or impure spirits. The New Testament writers distinguish carefully between people who are suffering from mental distress and people who are under spiritual oppression. Does your culture generally believe that demons exist and that this kind of oppression is possible? How would you explain the spiritual deliverance that Mark describes Jesus bringing to people who are under the controlling influence of demons?

4 Jesus performs his healings and exorcisms in a way that announces that God also wants people to be free from the restrictive traditions that have grown up around the law. When Jesus heals Simon's mother-in-law, he violates the rules that applied to rabbis of the time by taking a woman by the hand and receiving her hospitality. He also breaks a taboo against touching lepers. And he performs both the exorcism in the synagogue and the healing at Simon's home on the Sabbath, when no one was supposed to work. (The crowds wait until after sunset, when the Sabbath has ended, before they come for healing.) Even though Jesus is completely observant of the law in its true intentions (he tells the leper, for example, to offer the sacrifices Moses commanded for his ritual cleansing), he will soon come into sharp conflict with the religious teachers, who see their later confining traditions as part and parcel of the law. This conflict is foreshadowed in the brief reference to John the Baptist being put in prison. In classic storytelling fashion, Mark will provide the details of John's arrest later, after piquing our interest with this ominous notice here.

> ⊃ Are there traditions and taboos regarding clothing, food and drink, observance of particular days, interactions with other people, etc. that you were told are an essential aspect of following Jesus, but which you've since abandoned? If so, describe for the group how you decided that these things weren't essentials.

5 A final characteristic of Jesus' ministry is its paradoxical attempt at secrecy. Even though Jesus is the herald of God's arriving kingdom, he doesn't seem to want anyone to know this. He warns the leper, "See that you don't tell this to anyone." The spirit Jesus casts out in the synagogue is even able to identify him as "the Holy One of God," but Jesus forces it to be silent. However, these attempts at secrecy are ultimately unsuccessful. Word about Jesus spreads far and wide, and people flock to him from everywhere.

Mark actually wants the reader to wonder why Jesus would make an attempt at secrecy when he has come with such an important message and the attempt is futile anyway. The answer is that who Jesus truly is can't be revealed within the narrative until it becomes clear *in what way* he is who he is. What kind of Messiah is he? In what sense is he the Son of God? The first question will be answered at the end of Act III, when Simon (Peter) affirms he is the Messiah and Jesus then explains how he must suffer and be killed and rise again. The second question will be answered near the end of Act VI, when the Roman centurion, after seeing how Jesus dies, declares, "Surely this man was the Son of God!" In the meantime the characters within the narrative (and readers looking on with them) are left largely, but not entirely, in the dark, wondering about Jesus' identity. The impure spirit tells the crowd in the synagogue precisely who he is, but since this information comes from an untrustworthy source, they don't know what to make of it. Dramatic irony at its best.

> ⮕ What kinds of things might you say accurately about Jesus that would likely be misunderstood by the typical person in your culture until they had the chance to observe Jesus at work for some time in the lives of his followers?

SESSION 4

THE RELIGIOUS LEADERS CHALLENGE JESUS' TEACHINGS AND ACTIVITIES

Gospel of Mark > Part One > Act I: Jesus and the Religious Teachers, concluded

INTRODUCTION

As Jesus continues to teach and heal, he comes into open conflict with the religious teachers and their interpretation of the law. They challenge and question him, ultimately accusing him of blasphemy and lawbreaking. As Mark records how Jesus defends himself against their attacks, he gives us our first glimpse into the distinctive content of Jesus' teaching.

Act I ends with the religious teachers reaching a conclusion about who Jesus is: They decide he's someone so dangerous and subversive he has to be eliminated. But Jesus' ministry on earth will continue for some time before these leaders execute their plot, as Mark indicates in a closing summary of his activities.

In this summary there's another furtive reminder of the true identity of Jesus, as the demons cry out, "You are the Son of God" before Jesus silences them. But in these closing episodes of Act I Jesus also describes himself by another title, the Son of Man. This expression comes from a vision the prophet Daniel had of "one like a son of man" who was given "authority, glory and sovereign power" by God. Jesus chooses this expression to describe himself because it communicates his divine mission without having the nationalistic and militaristic overtones of some of the other titles that were used for the Messiah at this time (such as "Son of David," which he'll be called later in the book). The title Son of Man particularly highlights the humanity and humility of Jesus. He will invoke this title repeatedly in the second part of the gospel as he speaks of his coming sufferings and death. But here it captures the authority he has, as a divinely appointed representative of humanity, to forgive sins and determine how to make appropriate use of the Sabbath.

READING

Read the remaining episodes of Act I of Mark out loud like a play, beginning with "A few days later, when Jesus again entered Capernaum" and ending with "But he gave them strict orders not to tell others about him." Have people take these parts:
- Narrator
- Jesus
- Teachers of the law/Pharisees (the same spokesperson in each episode)
- People who question Jesus about fasting

DISCUSSION

1 Jesus wants people to understand the general principles behind God's laws and then freely determine the implications of those principles for their own lives. His rule for conduct on the Sabbath, for example, is that it is a day to do good and save life. Whatever meets this test is lawful. The teachers of the law, by contrast, have developed a maze of regulations that minutely classify countless actions as lawful or unlawful. Because their approaches are so different, Jesus considers the Sabbath a perfect occasion to heal the man with the shriveled hand, while the Pharisees are so outraged when he does this that they decide he must be destroyed.

➲ If you're a follower of Jesus, which do you tend to use, rules or general principles, to determine what words and actions honor him? If you've been using rules, can the example of Jesus here help you begin to discern what principles lie behind these rules, and to use those instead? Is that something you'd like to do?

2 Jesus often responds to his opponents by arguing, within the framework of general principles, from the greater to the lesser: If a more extreme statement or action is demonstrably in keeping with certain principles, then a corresponding but less extreme one should be as well.

Jesus uses this kind of argument to defend his disciples against the charge that they're breaking the law of Moses by plucking and eating heads of grain while traveling through a field. The law actually allows travelers to do this, so long as they don't carry any uneaten grain away in containers. But the Pharisees consider this to be harvesting—work that isn't permitted on the Sabbath. Jesus, as we've just seen, regards the Sabbath as a day to do good, so a simple activity that provides refreshment to weary travelers is clearly a lawful pursuit. To demonstrate this, he cites the more extreme example of David, who, "when he and his companions were hungry and in need," ate consecrated bread that only priests were supposed to eat. God never punished David for this. From Jesus' perspective, this was because the purpose of any kind of bread is to nourish hungry people, so it was appropriate for even this special bread to meet that need on an exceptional occasion. If David could break the actual law in such a flagrant way, so long as he was honoring God's basic intentions, then the disciples can certainly engage in an activity that the law permits, in order to fulfill the intentions of the Sabbath, even if this doesn't fit the Pharisees' particular interpretation.

Jesus uses a similar argument to demonstrate that he has the authority to forgive sins. He points out that it's easy to tell a paralytic that his sins are forgiven, since anyone can make that claim and there's no way to prove or disprove it. It's much harder to authoritatively command a paralytic to get up and walk, since it will be immediately obvious whether the speaker has that authority. If Jesus can make the man walk—the greater challenge—then it should be accepted that he can authoritatively forgive his sins as well.

➲ What tangible, observable things has God done in your life that give you the confidence he has also accomplished the intangible spiritual things he's promised you?

➲ Jesus heals the paralyzed man when he "sees the faith" of his friends. Faith in this sense means a confident expectation that God will act, expressed in bold initiative. To appreciate what this is like, re-create this story from the perspective of one of the friends who carries the man up onto the roof and lowers him down to Jesus. Have a volunteer portray this friend and have some other group members serve as a "media scrum" and conduct an interview about the experience, asking questions that arise from your consideration of this passage.

✖ Have you ever been prompted by faith (confident expectation of God's action) to take a daring course yourself? If so, what happened? Did your faith have effects in the lives of other people, as in this episode?

3 A final characteristic of Jesus' teaching is his use of analogies from earthly life to illustrate principles of the spiritual life. He does this in response to criticism that he eats with tax collectors and sinners and in response to a question about why his disciples don't fast (that is, go without food as a spiritual practice). Jesus may be quoting popular proverbs, perhaps adapting them to the immediate situation, or he may be inventing sayings of his own. Either way, this aspect of his teaching identifies both nature and culture as sources of potential insights into God's ways for those who can discern spiritual principles and recognize how they are illustrated in the world around them.

➲ Pick one of the following sayings and share with the group how you could follow the principle it illustrates in your life right now.

- "It is not the healthy who need a doctor, but the sick."
- "How can the guests of the bridegroom fast while he is with them?"
- "No one sews a patch of unshrunk cloth on an old garment."
- "No one pours new wine into old wineskins."

➲ What are some of your favorite sayings that illustrate spiritual principles through the worlds of nature or culture? (If you wish, think about this during the week ahead and share your sayings at the start of your group's next meeting.)

SESSION 5

JESUS APPOINTS TWELVE DISCIPLES, AND HIS FAMILY JOINS THE OPPOSITION

Gospel of Mark > Part One > Act II: Jesus and His Family and Neighbors

INTRODUCTION

Act II in the gospel of Mark shows how Jesus' family and neighbors responded to him. It's structured a little differently from Act I. That act first depicted Jesus teaching, healing and casting out demons with authority, and then it introduced the religious teachers and showed how they came into conflict with him. By contrast, Act II introduces Jesus' relatives right at the start, but they then fade into the background as Mark resumes his depiction of Jesus' teaching and miraculous powers. The relatives come back into view at the end of Act II, and their response to Jesus is to be understood in light of the events Mark has narrated and the themes he's developed throughout the whole act.

As we've noted, each of the three acts in the first part of Mark begins with a scene of Jesus engaging his disciples. Previously he has called various individuals to follow him; the callings of Peter, Andrew, James, John and Levi have been given as examples. Jesus now gathers a select group of his followers and chooses twelve of them to "be with him," that is, to observe his work closely so he can eventually send them out to proclaim the coming kingdom.

The next scene is one of the many places where Mark begins one story but then tells another before finishing the first one. This technique has a strategic purpose. Mark first reports that Jesus' family wants to come "take charge of him" because they think he's out of his mind. But Mark doesn't describe what happens when the family arrives until after he relates how some teachers of the law came from Jerusalem and accused Jesus of being demon possessed. The suspense that the audience feels about the family creates an interest in them, and this introduces the overall concern of this act. In this way the scene provides an artful transition from the theme of Act I to the theme of Act II, as both themes are represented in its various characters.

READING

Read the first two episodes of Act II out loud like a play, beginning with "Jesus went up on a mountainside" and ending with "Whoever does God's will is my brother and sister and mother." Have people take these parts:

- Narrator
- Jesus' family
- Teachers of the law from Jerusalem
- Jesus
- The crowd

DISCUSSION

1 Mark doesn't give us much information about the twelve people Jesus chose to "be with him" besides their names, but we have some hints that they were a diverse and boisterous group.

Simon the Zealot belonged to a movement that advocated violent struggle against the Roman occupation of the land. If, as many interpreters believe, Matthew is another name for Levi the tax collector, who was collaborating with the Romans, then the group included people from opposing ends of the political spectrum.

Mark records that Jesus gave James and John the name *Boanerges,* meaning "sons of thunder." This is likely a reference to their impetuous personalities, which we'll see on display later in the gospel. (Mark explains the meaning of this Aramaic term, which he has transliterated roughly into Greek, because he doesn't expect his Roman audience to understand Aramaic.) Jesus also gave Simon the name Peter, meaning "rock" in Greek. Mark doesn't indicate why Jesus chose this name; readers of his gospel might attribute it to anything from a steady personality to a chunky build. However, other gospel writers explain that the name captured the bedrock quality of Peter's faith in Jesus.

Beyond divergent political views and varying personalities, the group was also characterized by different degrees of actual loyalty to Jesus. Mark ominously notes that Judas Iscariot later betrayed him. (He uses the same term, meaning "to give over," as in his earlier reference to John the Baptist being "put in prison." Even in this first part of the gospel Mark is foreshadowing how the story will end.)

> The new names Jesus gives some of his disciples reflect their new role as his close collaborators. (As the gospel progresses, Jesus will allow these three renamed disciples, Peter, James and John, to witness the most important events of his ministry.) Do you know someone who has expressed their relationship to Jesus through an actual new name, or else through an email address, Twitter handle, blog name or something similar? Have you done this yourself? If so, what name have you chosen, and why?

> Jesus picked people with strong personalities from diverse backgrounds to form a ministry team. A team like this is at high risk for conflict. Why do you think Jesus took this risk, particularly when he and his followers were already under growing pressure from their opponents?

2 These teachers of the law have most likely come from Jerusalem in response to reports from their local counterparts, who have been watching Jesus closely. Jesus replies to the charge that he's possessed by Beelzebul, another name for Satan, with more of his characteristic analogies. (Mark now identifies these as "parables"; you'll explore their meaning and method in the next session.) Jesus shows that it's absurd to think Satan would undermine his own interests by casting out demons who are working for him. The real situation must be that Jesus has overpowered Satan and is now plundering his holdings.

Jesus warns these teachers of the law that by attributing the work the Holy Spirit is doing through him to Satan, they are at risk of blaspheming the Holy Spirit. This is an "eternal sin" that can "never be forgiven." Jesus doesn't mean that if people say or think certain things, they will be damned forever. Rather, he means that by considering the influence of the Holy Spirit something to be resisted rather than embraced, these teachers are putting themselves in a position where they can't, by definition, be saved, because they will never respond to the divine influences that are trying to draw them to salvation.

> ◯ Have you, or has someone you know, ever become concerned about committing the unpardonable sin that Jesus talks about here? If so, does this explanation reassure you? What do you think of the following statement? "If you're concerned that you've committed the unpardonable sin, you haven't, because your concern shows that you're still open to God's gracious influences."

3 When Jesus' family comes to take charge of him (literally to "seize" him, against his will), the delegation isn't led by his father. Most interpreters agree that this is because his father has died by this point. Instead, his mother and brothers come for him. But they're blocked from reaching him by the overflow crowd. When they send word to Jesus, he's not going to go outside and let himself be seized. But he goes much further than simply eluding them; he publicly repudiates his loyalty to them in favor of loyalty to a new family of the kingdom. He looks at the people who are "seated in a circle around him" and declares that they, not the relatives waiting outside, are his mother and brothers. (Mark states the contrast succinctly through a wordplay in Greek, contrasting those who are *peri* Jesus, around him, with those who are *para* Jesus, related to him.)

This circle most likely consists of the whole group of Jesus' close followers, not just the twelve disciples Jesus selected, since it includes women as well as men: Jesus says that anyone who does the will of God is his brother *and sister* and mother. He chose only men for the group who would eventually go out and proclaim the kingdom on their own, because such an activity would not have been permitted to women in this culture. But here we see that a wider group of close followers, which included women, actually traveled about with Jesus. (These followers may be the ones who later travel in the "other boats" when Jesus crosses the lake with his disciples. We'll see more evidence that women were in this group later in the gospel.)

➲ What's your reaction to the way Jesus makes a special point here of acknowledging his women followers as his sisters in the family of the kingdom?

➲ It's possible that many of the Roman believers this gospel is addressing had family members who thought they were out of their minds to risk their lives for Jesus. These family members may even have wanted to seize these believers and carry them off so they wouldn't take a public stand for their faith. If this is so, then the experience of Jesus here is vitally instructive for Mark's original audience. It remains so for believers today. If you're a follower of Jesus, how does your family feel about your faith? Have you ever had to risk losing their understanding, approval and even acceptance to follow Jesus loyally? If they have rejected you, have you found a new family among Jesus' followers that has restored some of the sense of belonging you've lost?

SESSION 6

JESUS TELLS PARABLES ABOUT HIS MESSAGE, HIS IDENTITY, AND THE KINGDOM OF GOD

Gospel of Mark > Part One > Act II: Jesus and His Family and Neighbors, continued

INTRODUCTION

Mark has already noted that when the teachers of the law challenged Jesus, he spoke to them in parables. What is a parable? In terms of its *form*, it's a comparison. (The Greek word *parabolē* means one thing set alongside another; Jesus introduces one of his parables by asking, "What shall we say the kingdom of God is like?") But in terms of its *purpose*, a parable is a kind of teaching that allows people to receive as much as they're ready for, without antagonizing them by demanding they accept things that are still beyond them.

Now Mark records a number of the parables that Jesus used to teach the crowds that gathered around him. He doesn't include these parables just to illustrate Jesus' teaching. Their message is vital to answer several questions that will be on readers' minds by this point in the gospel:

- Why have people been responding to Jesus in such different ways? While great crowds are coming to him eagerly, the religious leaders and his own relatives are hostile to him.
- Are people ever going to recognize who Jesus really is?
- Where's this kingdom of God that Jesus said was about to arrive? No cosmic, earth-shaking events have occurred yet.

Here in the middle of Act II, which is also the middle of the first part of the gospel, Mark takes a step back from the narrative and presents a concentrated block of Jesus' teaching—a collection of his parables—to address these concerns.

Mark notes that through his parables, Jesus taught the crowds "as much as they could understand." But Jesus also explained the deeper meaning of his teachings to his circle of close followers, expecting them to be ready for more.

READING

Have someone take the part of the narrator and read the introduction to this group of parables (beginning with "Again Jesus began to teach by the lake"), the explanation of the first parable, and the conclusion, ending with "But when he was alone with his own disciples, he explained everything."

Between the narrator's parts, have four other people read the four parables in this section, beginning at these places:

- "Listen! A farmer went out to sow his seed."
- "Do you bring in a lamp to put it under a bowl or a bed?"
- "This is what the kingdom of God is like. A man scatters seed on the ground."
- "What shall we say the kingdom of God is like . . . ? It is like a mustard seed."

DISCUSSION

1 The first parable in this section explains why Jesus has been getting such a mixed reception. The seed represents his message, and the different kinds of soil into which it falls represent the different states of the hearts of the people who are hearing the message. Some hearts, like those of the religious leaders, are hardened, so the message doesn't penetrate. Others embrace the message eagerly at first, but when they encounter trouble or persecution, "they quickly fall away." (Literally, "they are *scandalized*," that is, their moral sense is offended—this isn't what they signed up for!) Still others' hearts are so crowded with various desires that the message, even when embraced, gets choked. But a final group of hearts is open and sincere, and in them the message can take root and grow unencumbered. This group includes the circle of Jesus' close followers, whom Mark describes here as "the Twelve and the others around (*peri*) Jesus."

> ⊃ If a person in your culture is hearing the good news about Jesus but isn't initially open to it, what kinds of things can come along and carry the good news away in a torrent of distraction, like the birds on the path in Jesus' parable? List as many things as you can. (There are some suggestions at the end of this session that you can compare your list with once you've made it.)

> ⊃ If a person decided at first to follow Jesus with great enthusiasm, but was "scandalized" and gave up after only a short time when trouble or persecution came, what do you think they believed they were signing up for when they decided to follow Jesus? Where do people get such beliefs?

> ⊃ In your culture, what specific forms do the "worries of life," the "deceitfulness of wealth" and the "desires for other things" take? What measures can a person who sincerely wants to follow Jesus take to keep these things from choking off their faith?

> ⊃ When the word of God "produces a crop" in someone's life, this means both that their character is transformed and that they have an influence on many people around them. Describe for the group someone whose character and faith influenced you to consider following Jesus.

2 When Jesus explains this parable to his close followers, it may appear that he doesn't want "those on the outside" to understand, since he says that when they listen, they will be "ever seeing but never perceiving" and "ever hearing but never understanding." However, Jesus is actually quoting from the book of Isaiah here. This is how God described what the response of the hard-hearted Israelites would be when he sent Isaiah to speak to them. These words explain what happens to someone whose heart is like the first kind of soil. But it's clear from this parable that other kinds of responses are possible. It's even clearer from the next parable that Jesus wants everyone to understand. He uses a lamp to illustrate that he's not deliberately concealing the truth about himself. He wants this to be "brought out into the open," and ultimately it will be. And so, he tells his listeners—most likely the entire crowd once again—"Consider carefully what you hear." If people don't understand, it's not because God doesn't want them to, it's because of how they're listening.

➲ Jesus says that the way we listen to his message will inevitably result in our having either more or less understanding. How can hearing more lead to understanding less?

➲ Can you give an example of someone who has heard a lot about Jesus but who doesn't appear to have understood much about him?

3 Jesus begins his final two parables, about how seed grows "all by itself" and about how the tiny mustard seed becomes the largest of plants, by saying he's going to describe what the kingdom of God is like. This kingdom was proclaimed with great fanfare at the beginning of Mark's gospel, but until now readers haven't heard anything else about it. Or perhaps they've been hearing about it all along. Jesus explains through these two parables that while the kingdom begins in tiny, obscure ways and expands largely unnoticed, eventually its scope will become worldwide. (The birds perching in the branches are a symbol drawn from the Hebrew prophets that represents other nations coming under the influence of Israel's faith.) The events Mark has been relating, which have been taking place in the obscure province of Galilee, far from the Roman Empire's centers of knowledge and power, will eventually reshape the world. This is the secret of the kingdom of God, which can already be shared with those who have open hearts.

➲ Where do you see the kingdom of God growing around you, perhaps in ways that don't seem earth-shaking in themselves, but which represent the expansion of God's influence in your society and in the lives of its people?

Suggestions for discussion point 1, question 1: Things that can distract a person from paying attention to the good news about Jesus include, among other things, a romantic interest in someone who discourages faith in Jesus, the disapproval of parents and other family members, the influence of friends, cynical and skeptical messages in the media, and college and university courses that disparage or ridicule faith.

SESSION 7

JESUS CALMS A STORM AND DRIVES OUT A LEGION OF DEMONS

Gospel of Mark > Part One > Act II: Jesus and His Family and Neighbors, continued

INTRODUCTION

Once he has finished teaching the crowd in parables, Jesus decides to go to the other side of the lake (the Sea of Galilee), into a region inhabited by Gentiles. Jesus wants to get away for a while from the large crowds that are pressing upon him. (He had to deliver his parables from a boat because so many people were massed on the lake shore.) But the trip also helps Mark develop some important themes. For one thing, he wants to illustrate for his Roman audience how Jesus brought the good news of the kingdom to Gentiles like themselves. Beyond this, Jesus does two remarkable miracles during this journey across the lake, which his relatives and neighbors will soon hear about, forcing them to confront the question of his identity. Finally, the two episodes on this journey also highlight Mark's key themes of faith and fear. There have been hints of them earlier in the gospel, but now they come into sharp focus. They will be crucial to the development of Act II and the message of the gospel as a whole.

READING

Read the next two episodes of Act II out loud like a play, beginning with "That day when evening came, he said to his disciples, 'Let us go over to the other side'" and ending with "And all the people were amazed." Have people take these parts:

- Narrator
- Jesus
- Disciples
- Legion, the impure spirit(s)

When you get to the second episode, if you wish, you can have the actors pantomime the events while the narrator reads, instead of speaking their separate parts. For example, the person who portrays the man with the impure spirit can hold up imaginary chains and then show how he can break them, he can fall on his knees before Jesus, etc. (If you have improvisational actors in your group, this is their chance to shine!)

DISCUSSION

1 When Jesus calms the storm on the lake, this reveals a further aspect of his power and authority: "Even the wind and the waves obey him!" This makes the disciples ask even more urgently, "Who is this?" But Jesus has a question for them that's just as urgent, because their response will ultimately determine their ability to recognize and follow him: "Why are you so *afraid*? Do you still have no *faith*?"

As we saw in the case of the friends of the paralyzed man, the kind of faith Jesus is referring to here is a confident expectation that God will act, expressed in bold initiative. Faith is kingdom involvement. It's the good soil in which the seed grows and yields a great harvest. The opposite of this faith is fear, which expresses itself in doubt and inactivity. Fear is choosing not to become involved in the kingdom. In fear, the disciples respond to the deadly peril they're facing by questioning whether Jesus cares about them. (Similarly, the people of the Gerasene region plead with Jesus to leave their region, because they're afraid.) Mark will note further responses of faith and fear as his gospel continues, and the whole work will culminate in a stark contrast between faith and fear that will show readers they must choose one or the other.

> ⤷ Where does God want you to take bold initiative to become involved in the work of his kingdom? What fears would keep you from doing this? Respond in faith to each of these fears by reminding yourself who Jesus is and how he is able to help you, based on what you've seen so far in the gospel of Mark. (For example, "Jesus cares about me," "Jesus calms the storms," "Jesus can help me understand God's ways," etc.) Continue to build your faith by noting more of Jesus' qualities and abilities in the sessions ahead.

2 Even though Jesus has crossed the lake to get a break from the crowds, he continues to face dramatic challenges. After he calms the storm and lands safely on the opposite shore, he's immediately confronted by a potent force of demons concentrated in the body of a single victim. They engage Jesus in a power contest. When he commands them to leave the man, they try to take spiritual authority over him. They believe that if they can address him by name ("Jesus, Son of the Most High God") and bind him with an oath ("In God's name"), they'll bring him under their control. But all of their measures are powerless. Jesus forces them to disclose their own name instead—it's Legion, the term for a large group of Roman soldiers—and he casts them out of the man.

> ⤷ Have you ever heard of a situation in which a curse or spell was powerless against a follower of Jesus, who overcame it in his name? If so, share the story with the group. If this is outside your experience, what do you make of such stories?

3 In what they think is a successful negotiation, the demons get permission to remain in this inhabited area, where they expect to find more victims, by going temporarily into a nearby herd of pigs. But this is such a shock to the pigs that they rush down the hillside and are drowned in the lake. It's not clear what happens to the demons, but they certainly don't get what they bargained for.

➲ Many readers of this account are troubled by the way Jesus allows the people of this region to suffer a huge economic loss through the destruction of this great herd of livestock. What would you say in response to these concerns? If the demons were killed by drowning or if they had to leave the region for lack of a host, would the population be better off in the end? Would this justify the destruction of their property and livelihood?

4 To this point Jesus has typically ordered people not to tell anyone when he heals or delivers them. But Jesus tells this man to go home to his own people and share with them what the Lord has done for him. The difference may be that here in Gentile territory there is less risk of misunderstanding who Jesus is: The man's friends and relatives aren't expecting a nationalistic and militaristic Messiah.

In other words, Jesus recognizes that it's better not to know something than to think you know something when you don't. It's much easier to learn than to unlearn. The people back on Jesus' home side of the lake have the problem of unlearning. They can't be told he is the Messiah until they understand what kind of Messiah he actually is. The people on this side of the lake are free to hear with amazement about his power and mercy. We'll see how they respond to this man's testimony when Jesus returns to this area later in the gospel.

But there's also a certain irony about Jesus' suggestion that the people who know this man the best will be most able to appreciate what God has done for him. This won't be true in Jesus' own case. When he comes back across the lake and returns to his own hometown, the people there will reject him.

➲ What things have you had to work hardest to unlearn in order to understand better and better who Jesus is?

➲ If you're a follower of Jesus, which people have been best able to appreciate God's work in your life, "your own people" from your family and hometown, or others who've only met you later in life? Explain why.

SESSION 8

JESUS DOES TWO MORE GREAT MIRACLES, BUT HE'S REJECTED IN HIS HOMETOWN

Gospel of Mark > Part One > Act II: Jesus and His Family and Neighbors, concluded

INTRODUCTION

On his trip across the lake Jesus demonstrated his power over the forces of nature and concentrated demonic opposition. Now on his return he shows his power over illness that no one can cure and even over death itself. All of this leads up to the culmination of Act II, when Jesus returns to his hometown of Nazareth and his family and neighbors are confronted with the question of his identity in light of the remarkable miracles they're hearing about.

READING

Read the closing episodes of Act II out loud like a play, beginning with "When Jesus had again crossed over by boat to the other side of the lake" and ending with "He was amazed at their lack of faith." Have people take these parts:

- Narrator
- Jairus, the synagogue leader
- The woman suffering from bleeding
- Jesus

- Disciples
- People from Jairus's house
- People in Nazareth

DISCUSSION

1 This is another place where Mark begins one story and then relates a second one before finishing the first. This technique once again creates suspense that focuses the audience on an element Mark wants to highlight. Jairus's daughter is dying, so the delay Jesus experiences on his way to help her intensifies the threat of death and ultimately emphasizes Jesus' power over death. The two stories also work together on a narrative level. Jairus needs great faith to believe that Jesus can help him even after his daughter has died, and he can find encouragement in the bold faith he's just seen the woman demonstrate.

In fact, Mark uses the turning point at the center of these intertwined episodes to underscore the themes of faith and fear that he's been developing. The woman is ceremonially unclean in her condition, so it's a ritual infraction for her to touch Jesus. When he starts looking for her, she trembles with *fear* of exposure and possible punishment. Nevertheless, even though she has already disappeared into the crowd, she returns and identifies herself, and Jesus assures her that her *faith* has healed her. (And as in the case of the leper, Jesus isn't worried about traditional taboos; he sends her away in peace.)

When, immediately afterward, messengers tell Jairus that his daughter is dead, Jesus responds, "Don't be *afraid*; just *believe*"—that is, have *faith*. (The English words "believe" and "faith" translate the same Greek root.) Mark has been steadily developing the contrast between the responses of fear and faith—turning away from the kingdom or engaging with it—and now he presents the choice between them in stark relief. This is the choice that Jesus' family and neighbors will soon face.

⤷ Imagine that the woman who's been healed goes to the synagogue to worship on the next Sabbath. Jairus, who's a synagogue leader, recognizes her there. In gratitude for the inspiration her faith provided to him when he needed it most, he and his wife invite her to come to their home for a meal and meet their daughter. Picture the conversation between the woman and Jairus at this meal. What kinds of things do they ask one another? Write up the conversation between them and have two of your group members perform it as a dramatic dialogue for the rest of the group (or for your whole church if you're using this guide for a community Bible experience).

⊃ The woman recognizes the approach of the kingdom of God in the person of Jesus and demonstrates confident faith through the action of reaching out to touch him. This draws out power in a way that even Jesus must work to understand. Have you ever taken an initiative for the kingdom in confident faith and seen this dramatically attract God's power? If so, share your story with the group.

⊃ Jesus healed and delivered people to declare that God's kingdom was approaching, but he didn't make a complete end of disease and death. Do you know someone who's strong in faith but who is nevertheless living with a lifelong illness or coping with the loss of a child? How are they dealing with this? What doubts and struggles do they have? How does their faith help them?

2 The people of Jesus' hometown are amazed by his teaching. They've also heard about the remarkable miracles he's been doing, and this has added to their amazement. Amazement has been the general response to Jesus. The people on the other side of the lake are amazed to see the demon-possessed man freed; Jairus and his relatives are completely astonished when his daughter is raised from the dead.

This amazement is inevitably the precursor to a decision, because the events that prompt it are too compelling to dismiss. Unfortunately, Jesus' relatives and neighbors choose to "take offense" at him. Literally, they're *scandalized*, just like the people represented by the second kind of soil in Jesus' parable. Because they see only superficially, their moral and religious sense is offended by the idea that a local boy would go around acting like a great man. And so they step away from the kingdom instead of embracing it.

At the end of this episode, Mark describes their response as a lack of *faith*. This draws together the themes he has developed in his accounts of Jesus' parables and miracles throughout Act II: When confronted with the kingdom in the person of Jesus, people respond based on the state of their hearts. Jesus expects the people of his hometown to respond in faith, given all they've seen and heard. When they don't, *he's* amazed.

> ⮕ This episode is the only place in the gospel where Mark says that Jesus couldn't do something: "He could not do any miracles there" because the people of his hometown lacked faith. We saw earlier that the exercise of bold faith attracts divine power; do you think people can restrict divine power by giving in to fear or taking offense? Explain.

> ⮕ If you've gotten discouraging results from a ministry initiative, could one possible explanation be that others didn't share the faith (the expectation that God would act) that led you to take this initiative? If so, does this recognition help you be less discouraged about your part, at least, in what happened?

SESSION 9

JESUS SENDS HIS DISCIPLES OUT, AND MARK REPORTS THE FATE OF JOHN THE BAPTIST

Gospel of Mark > Part One > Act III: Jesus and His Disciples

INTRODUCTION

In the first two acts of his gospel, Mark has depicted the Jewish religious teachers and Jesus' relatives and neighbors responding to the question of his identity. Now in Act III he will show Jesus' disciples responding to this question. Early in the act several possibilities are raised for who Jesus might be: Is he John the Baptist, returned from the dead? Is he Elijah? Is he a prophet like those of long ago? These same possibilities will be raised again at the very end of the act, but by then the disciples, represented by Peter, will know enough to assert that he is the Messiah. Repeatedly throughout the act Mark will comment on how much the disciples do and don't understand. Readers will recognize by the end that while the disciples do realize Jesus is the Messiah, they don't yet grasp what kind of Messiah he is. The second part of the gospel will explore that issue.

Act III begins, like the first two acts, with a scene of Jesus engaging his disciples. Previously he has called various individuals to follow him and he has appointed twelve of them to "be with him" and observe his ministry closely. Now this time of observation is over and Jesus continues the disciples' apprenticeship by sending them out to preach, heal and deliver on their own.

Mark then tells us at last what happened to John the Baptist when he was put in prison. The recounting of this story creates an interlude that represents the time the Twelve are away on their mission. But the story also serves several important thematic purposes. It raises the possibilities about Jesus' identity that are resolved at the end of Act III. It also demonstrates that Jesus has sent his followers out into a hostile and dangerous world—an important warning for Mark's Roman audience to take to heart. Finally, by contrast with surrounding episodes, the story dramatizes the difference between the values of God's kingdom and the ways of earthly kingdoms like Herod's.

READING AND DISCUSSION

1 Have someone read the account of Jesus sending out the Twelve, beginning with "Then Jesus went around teaching from village to village" and ending with "They drove out many demons and anointed many sick people with oil and healed them."

> ○ Jesus allows his disciples to take some very basic clothing and equipment with them, but for the most part this mission is supposed to be an exercise of faith, based on the confident expectation that God will provide for them and work through them as they step out in obedience. What's the closest thing you've ever done to what the disciples do here? Did you see God act as you expected?

> ○ The disciples must be prepared for opposition; some places won't welcome them or listen to them. Jesus tells them in those cases simply to give an ominous warning and move on to a more receptive audience. What are the signs that show us that we've done all we can to challenge a person or group to follow Jesus and that we need to move on, at least until they're better able to hear and understand what we're saying?

2 Have someone read the story of Herod and John the Baptist, beginning with "King Herod heard about this, for Jesus' name had become well known" and ending with "On hearing of this, John's disciples came and took his body and laid it in a tomb."

Herod rules Galilee (the province in which Jesus has been active) on behalf of the Romans, but his heritage is Jewish. For that reason, and to avoid antagonizing his mostly Jewish subjects, Herod generally observes the Jewish law. But he breaks the law very publicly by marrying his living brother's ex-wife. (Historians tell us that while Herodias couldn't have divorced Philip under Jewish law, she used her Roman citizenship to do this under Roman law.) When John the Baptist criticizes the action, Herod imprisons him, but he doesn't execute him as Herodias wishes because he knows that John is a "righteous and holy man." Nevertheless, Herodias gets her chance on Herod's birthday. Knowing that her husband is likely to promise an extravagant reward for pleasing entertainment, she sends her daughter to dance at the banquet. Sure enough, Herod makes an offer that ultimately forces him to execute John even though he doesn't want to.

Mark tells this story to explain what happened to John and to foreshadow what will similarly happen to Jesus. (Jesus' opponents, the Pharisees, have already consulted with Herod's supporters about how to destroy him, and Jesus will later warn his disciples about the danger of both groups.) But Mark also uses the story to contrast life in the kingdom of God with life in kingdoms like Herod's. Significantly, Mark describes Herodias's daughter with the term *korasion*, meaning a girl who is just reaching the age of betrothal, when a marriage can be arranged for her. He uses the same term for Jairus's twelve-year-old daughter. (Women in this culture married in their early teens.) But these are the only two characters in the gospel who are described by this term. The juxtaposition of the accounts in which they appear draws a significant contrast.

Jairus's daughter is cared for by loving parents; through their faith, she becomes a means of displaying God's mercy and power. Herodias's daughter is exploited by both her mother and her stepfather, and she becomes a means of thwarting God's kingdom. Herod exploits her sexuality by having her dance before his male guests, even though she's his niece and stepdaughter. Herodias exploits her sexuality by making it the lure for an impetuous promise through which she wins her contest with her husband over John's fate. In Herod's kingdom people of power and privilege use others as pawns, destroying lives as they pursue their own ambitions. What clearer case could be made for giving one's loyalty to the kingdom Jesus is proclaiming, even if this means risk and danger, rather than to someone like Herod—or Caesar?

➲ Herod recognizes that John the Baptist is a righteous and holy man and he likes to listen to him. But when he does, he's "greatly puzzled." He can't make sense of what John is saying. Why do you think he can't?

➲ What options did Herod have in responding to his stepdaughter's request, besides executing John the Baptist on the spot? (There's a suggestion at the end of this session that you can consider after you've thought about Herod's options on your own.) Why do you think Herod didn't take any of the other options that were open to him?

➲ In the best tradition of the Hebrew prophets, John the Baptist speaks truth to power. But as a result, he becomes a pawn in the intrigues of this manipulative and exploitive ruling family. In the end, John pays with his life. Do you think the kingdom of God was advanced through his sacrifice? If so, how? If not, why not?

➲ In light of this passage, can you recognize some other situations in which people in positions of worldly power have used manipulation and exploitation to advance their own interests instead of God's? If so, what people and situations come to mind?

Suggestion for discussion point 2, question 2: Herod could have said, "I'm sorry, but John the Baptist's head isn't mine to give you. He needs to be tried under Roman law and only executed if he's found guilty. But ask for anything that is mine to give you, and it's yours."

SESSION 10

JESUS FEEDS FIVE THOUSAND PEOPLE AND WALKS ON THE WATER

Gospel of Mark > Part One > Act III: Jesus and His Disciples, continued

INTRODUCTION

Having described the fate of John the Baptist, Mark now finishes the story about what happened when Jesus sent the twelve disciples out to teach, heal and deliver. Mark's main concern here in Act III is with the disciples' understanding of Jesus, so they'll be central figures in the narrative for the rest of this act.

The disciples' need for a time of rest after their mission prompts Jesus to lead them across the lake to a solitary place. This sets in motion a series of events that results in Jesus doing two further remarkable miracles. These have a symbolic significance that reveals something important about who Jesus is. But the disciples now have an obstacle to their understanding that they'll need to overcome before they can get the message.

READING

Read the next episode in Act III out loud like a play, beginning with "The apostles gathered around Jesus and reported to him all they had done and taught" and ending with "The number of the men who had eaten was five thousand." Have people take these parts:

- Narrator
- Jesus
- The disciples

Then have someone read the next episode, beginning with "Immediately Jesus made his disciples get into the boat and go on ahead of him" and ending with "They begged him to let them touch even the edge of his cloak, and all who touched it were healed."

DISCUSSION

1 Mark has already contrasted the manipulative and exploitive interactions within Herod's family with the loving care shown by Jairus's family. He now contrasts the debauchery at Herod's birthday banquet with the simplicity, dignity and compassion at the feast Jesus creates in this immediately following episode.

Practical compassion has consistently accompanied Jesus' exercise of power. For example, he ensured that the man with leprosy and the woman afflicted with bleeding were restored to ceremonial cleanness and thus to community. When he raised Jairus's daughter from the dead, he told her family to give her something to eat. Now Jesus looks with compassion on the hungry crowds and, in a direct echo of those instructions, he tells his disciples, "You give them something to eat." But the resulting miracle expresses more than just God's desire to care for those in need. It also expresses his desire to welcome great crowds into his kingdom, embodied here in a feast that evokes the "Messianic banquet" that Jews of this period spoke of as a symbol for the time when God would establish his reign over all the world.

Later in the gospel we'll see Jesus institute the Lord's Supper as a way for his followers to express their faith in the coming of that time through the effects of his death. But this account anticipates the Lord's Supper, as Jesus takes the bread, gives thanks for it, blesses it and gives it to his disciples to distribute. Through a miracle of compassion, a spontaneous shared meal in a solitary place becomes, for a moment, an advance experience of the kingdom of God on earth.

➲ The disciples protest that what Jesus is asking them to do is way beyond their current resources. They haven't got half a year's wages. Jesus asks in response how much they do have. Have you felt God calling you to do something but you haven't responded because it seems way beyond your resources? What do you have? How could you offer this to God as a starting point? What might happen if you did?

➲ Jesus, in effect, serves the Lord's Supper at a picnic on the grass. What's the most informal or spontaneous way you've ever shared in the Lord's Supper? Have you ever had it as part of a full meal, as happens here? Tell the group about your experiences.

2 On the way back across the lake Jesus does another miracle that reveals more of his authority over the forces of nature. But taken together with the feeding of the five thousand, his walking on the water also discloses a vital aspect of his identity.

These two miracles echo the two great miracles of the exodus. When God brought the Israelites out of slavery in Egypt he provided food for them in the wilderness after making them walk safely through the Red Sea. Jesus, in other words, does the same kind of things that God did through Moses at the foundational moments of Israelite history. This points to his identity as the Son of God. The identification with Moses is heightened by Mark's reference to the crowds as "like sheep without a shepherd." This is an allusion to the First Testament. When God told Moses he was about to die, Moses asked him to raise up another leader in his place, "so the LORD's people will not be like sheep without a shepherd."

The disciples, however, aren't able to appreciate what these miracles reveal about Jesus. Mark explains that this is because "they had not understood about the loaves; their hearts were hardened." This is very strong language. Mark has only described one other group as having hardened hearts: the religious teachers who were watching Jesus to find a reason to accuse him. The expression describes people who have already reached a conclusion and so are not open to the implications of new information.

What conclusion have the disciples reached? Many interpreters believe that as a result of their own experiences of preaching, healing, and delivering, they've decided that Jesus is a man with a particular degree of spiritual authority and that they've now gotten a share of it themselves. If there's a difference between themselves and Jesus, it's just a matter of degree, not of kind. Seeing him multiply the loaves challenges this belief, so they don't factor this experience and its symbolic significance into their understanding of who he is. As a result, they're not thinking of Jesus as the divine Son of God, so they respond in fear and terror when they see him walking on the water—more evidence that he hasn't just got more of what they have, he's got something way beyond it.

> ➲ Straining at the oars against a contrary wind, the disciples can't make any progress no matter how hard they try. But Jesus can go right past them without even having a boat. What would be a hardhearted response to seeing something like this? What response do you think Jesus would like his followers to have instead?

> ➲ Which of the characters in the two accounts you read for this session do you most identify with at this point in your life? Why?

SESSION 11

JESUS DECLARES ALL FOODS CLEAN AND MINISTERS AMONG THE GENTILES

Gospel of Mark > Part One > Act III: Jesus and His Disciples, continued

INTRODUCTION

The Pharisees and teachers of the law now return to the story for the first time since Mark turned his focus from them to Jesus' family at the beginning of Act II. But here in the middle of Act III, the renewed conflict with these old opponents serves primarily to trigger a saying of Jesus that the disciples must work to understand: "Nothing outside a person can defile them by going into them. Rather, it is what comes out of a person that defiles them." Mark's focus remains on the disciples and their struggle to appreciate who Jesus is.

After his exchange with the Pharisees, Jesus heads into Gentile territory to get away from the crowds for a time, as he did when he sailed across the lake and met the man possessed by a legion of demons. Once again Jesus finds that God has assignments waiting for him in places outside his expected sphere of ministry.

As you read these episodes, notice how Mark continues to help his Roman audience understand events that are taking place in a distant culture by explaining Jewish customs and by translating Aramaic expressions such as *Corban* and *Ephphatha*.

Also notice how the image of bread, or more generally of food and eating, appears in various forms in most of the episodes here in Act III. In the ones you've already read, Jesus tells his disciples not to bring any bread with them (this can be easily provided!); Herod hosts a feast; Jesus breaks bread and feeds five thousand people; and the disciples "don't understand about the loaves." In the reading for this session, the Pharisees criticize the disciples for eating food (literally bread) with unclean hands, and Jesus and a Gentile woman exchange quips about bread and crumbs. Mark, a master storyteller, is using bread as a recurring metaphor for receiving God's blessings.

READING

Read the next three episodes in Act III out loud like a play, beginning with "The Pharisees and some of the teachers of the law who had come from Jerusalem gathered around Jesus" and ending with "'He has done everything well,' they said. 'He even makes the deaf hear and the mute speak.'" Have people take these parts:
- Narrator
- Pharisees and teachers of the law
- Jesus
- Woman in Tyre
- People of the Decapolis

DISCUSSION

1 As they did when they saw the disciples plucking heads of grain when traveling through a field, the Pharisees and teachers of the law once again protest that Jesus and his followers aren't keeping the traditional requirements that have grown up around the law. In this case their objection is that the disciples aren't living according to the "tradition of the elders" because they don't perform a ceremonial handwashing before eating. Jesus warns his opponents in response that if they place too much emphasis on their traditions, they may actually give them priority over the "commands of God."

He then gives an illustration of how they're already doing this. Jews of the time could declare certain possessions or resources to be *Corban*, effectively dedicating them to God with a vow that rendered them unavailable for normal uses. Apparently cases had arisen where adult children had told their parents that certain resources they might have counted on for support in their old age were *Corban* and not available to them. This brought two provisions of the law into conflict with one another. The Ten Commandments required children to provide for their parents ("honor your father and mother"), but another law forbade people to take back vows they'd made. The teachers of the law had expressed their opinion that keeping the vow took priority. This ruling was a human tradition that was now allowing people to disobey a commandment of God.

After giving this illustration, Jesus returns to the original issue of eating without performing a ceremonial handwashing. He addresses it through a broad statement that Mark identifies as a "parable," meaning a comparison (in this case between the effects of two different things). Jesus says that nothing can defile a person by going into them from the outside; rather, it's what comes out of a person that defiles them. Jesus introduces this parable with the formula, "Listen to me, everyone, and *understand* this." (This is similar to the formula that sometimes concludes his parables, "Whoever has ears to hear, let them hear.") Even so, the disciples have to ask Jesus to explain the statement. This shows that they are "without understanding" (NIV "dull"). Mark notes for his readers the broader effects of Jesus' sweeping declaration: It makes all foods clean. The principle behind it has even further implications that will become apparent in the next two episodes.

> ⊃ The parents of a college student are helping her with her tuition and living expenses. They're surprised and upset when they discover that she's been tithing their gifts (giving one tenth of them to her church and other ministries). They tell her to stop doing this because their gifts are meant to see their own child through college, not fund other activities. But she feels strongly that she should tithe all of her income. What would you advise her to do? Why?

2 Readers of the gospels are often disturbed by the way Jesus speaks to the woman who asks him to deliver her daughter from a demon: "It is not right to take the children's bread and toss it to the dogs." It's important to appreciate that what's happening here is the kind of verbal sparring that the people of these Mediterranean cultures loved to engage in, pitting one proverb against another until one speaker had prevailed. Jesus is likely quoting a popular saying to explain that he understands his mission to be essentially to his fellow Israelites. The woman wittily and persuasively enters the world of his saying and turns it on its head: "Even the dogs under the table eat the children's crumbs." "For such a reply," Jesus responds—in other words, "You've got me there"—you may have your wish.

Mark's readers, who've just heard about the feeding of the five thousand, know that the "children" (the Israelites) have already *eaten all they wanted* and that there are plenty of *crumbs* available for others. Through his exchange with the woman, Jesus comes to share this same insight. In the next episode, he'll help another Gentile without hesitation. Ceremonial cleanness truly is a matter of what's in a person's heart.

> ⮕ Can you give examples from your own culture of people sparring with proverbs, perhaps reworking them in the process? (For example, an employee arrives well after opening time and announces, "Better late than never." The employer responds, "Better never late.")

> ⮕ This episode contains Mark's most daring use of dramatic irony yet: Readers actually understand something before Jesus does. What do you think of Mark's portrayal of Jesus learning something here? Do you have a problem with it, because he's supposed to be omniscient? Or do you like the idea that Jesus has an open heart, not a hardened heart, and so he recognizes and embraces the implications of new information?

3 Jesus leaves Tyre but remains in Gentile territory, probably to continue taking a rest from the pressing crowds. He returns to the Decapolis, where the man he delivered from the legion of demons has told everyone about him. On his first visit the people *pleaded* with Jesus to leave their region; now they *beg* him (the same word in Greek) to heal a man who can't hear or speak. The man's testimony has transformed the attitude of the entire region.

One striking feature of this healing is the way Jesus spits on his fingers and then touches the man's tongue. While people in many cultures today might be uncomfortable with this, Jesus is using his saliva as an extension of himself. It's like when he lays hands on someone, or when they reach out and touch his clothing. Jesus first establishes a physical connection with the other person and then ministers God's healing power to them.

> Is there a physical medium that helps you connect with Jesus? (For example, a cross on the wall, a portrait of Jesus in your home or church, a treasured Bible, the bread and wine of communion, or the world of nature and creation?) Do you think Jesus wants to connect with you through means like these? For you and your community of believers, which is the greater danger: to let the means become an object of worship itself—an idol—or to dissociate Jesus too strongly from the physical world he had to enter to save us?

SESSION 12

THE IDENTITY OF JESUS COMES INTO FOCUS THROUGH A REPEATED SERIES OF EVENTS

Gospel of Mark > Part One > Act III: Jesus and His Disciples, concluded

INTRODUCTION

Since resuming his narrative after explaining what happened to John the Baptist, Mark has recounted episodes in which:

- Jesus feeds five thousand people in a remote place
- The disciples fail to understand about the loaves as they travel with Jesus by boat
- There's conflict with the Pharisees as they challenge Jesus
- Jesus delivers a woman's daughter and heals a man who is deaf

Now, as Mark draws Act III to a close, he relates four more episodes, in almost the same order, in which almost the same things happen:

- Jesus feeds four thousand people in a remote place
- There's conflict with the Pharisees as they challenge Jesus
- The disciples fail to understand about the loaves as they travel with Jesus by boat
- Jesus heals a man who is blind

What's going on here?

Mark isn't repeating himself accidentally. He hasn't found two different accounts of the same period in Jesus' life and decided to include them both because he's not sure which one is more accurate. Rather, like all of the New Testament authors who tell Jesus' story, Mark is choosing specific episodes to work into his gospel, and he's presenting them in a way that will best help his audience understand who Jesus is and how they need to follow him in their own place and time. Each of the incidents Mark relates comes authentically from the life of Jesus and has been passed down from those who saw and heard Jesus when he was alive on earth. (As we saw in session 1, Mark's primary source was most likely Peter himself.) But Mark adds much value in the telling as he relates this second series of events, as we'll now see. That's what it means for him to be an inspired author writing Scripture.

READING

Read the rest of Act III out loud like a play, beginning with "During those days another crowd gathered" and ending with "Jesus warned them not to tell anyone about him." Have people take these parts:

- Narrator
- Jesus
- Disciples
- Pharisees
- Blind man

As you read, notice how Mark continues to use bread as a metaphor for blessing and understanding.

DISCUSSION

1 Jesus is still in the Decapolis, ministering among Gentiles, when he performs his second miracle of multiplying food to feed thousands of people. Mark wants us to recognize the similarities between this miraculous feeding and the first one, so he relates the two stories in very much the same way: The question arises of how to feed so many in such a remote place; Jesus asks the disciples how many loaves they have; he has the crowd sit on the ground; he takes the loaves, gives thanks, breaks them and gives them to the disciples to distribute; many baskets of leftover pieces are gathered afterwards. Mark wants us to see these similarities because they show that the kingdom of God actually has enough blessings available for the Gentiles to be completely satisfied along with the people of Israel. They don't need to be content with just a few crumbs falling off the table.

So that we appreciate this truth, Mark also wants us to recognize the most important difference between the two stories: The crowd this time is made up of Gentiles and not Jews. So Mark uses a different term for basket in this account: *spuris*, the common Greek term for a woven container, instead of *kophinos*, a small basket of distinctively Jewish design, which he used in the account of the feeding of the five thousand. Some interpreters also see a significance in the difference between the numbers in the two accounts. Five loaves and five thousand people may signify the five books of Moses, and twelve baskets the twelve tribes of Israel, while four thousand people may represent the four corners of the earth and seven loaves and seven baskets the comprehensive scope of the salvation Jesus is bringing. It's possible that Mark is coloring the account with symbolic details like this, but it's more likely that these are the actual numbers and that Mark chooses to report them because they are so delightfully appropriate.

> ⊃ On this trip into Gentile territory Jesus and his disciples are being challenged to move into new spiritual territory. It's one thing to *say* that ceremonial cleanness is a matter of the heart. It's another thing (as Jesus recognizes) to *heal* the daughter of a Gentile woman. And now he and the disciples *eat* with Gentiles. This was something Jews weren't permitted to do at this time, but it symbolizes how the salvation Jesus is bringing is meant for people of every nation. If you've had a similar experience where God has challenged your categories and drawn you way out of your comfort zone, tell the group about it.

2 The Pharisees challenge Jesus to produce a "sign from heaven" (that is, from God) to authenticate his ministry. By "sign" they don't mean the kind of miracles he's already been doing, through which divine power has been meeting human needs. They mean a sign-on-demand whose only purpose is to prove that Jesus has been sent by God. Moses was able to do this kind of sign. He could, for example, throw his staff to the ground and turn it into a snake. The Pharisees are wondering whether Jesus can do the same kind of thing.

> ⊃ Do you think God would have given Jesus the power to do a sign like this if he'd asked? If so, why did Jesus refuse to give this kind of sign?

3 Jesus uses bread as a metaphor when he tells his disciples to "watch out for the yeast of the Pharisees and that of Herod." Jesus speaks literally of leaven, which made bread rise through a process of fermentation, and which was therefore also a symbol of infiltration and decay. Jesus is warning his disciples against the insidious corrupting influence of the Pharisees' hard hearts. But the disciples fail to understand. All they can imagine is that Jesus is scolding them for not bringing enough food along in the boat. This provides an opportunity for Jesus to remind them, and for Mark to remind his audience, of the twelve basketfuls (using the term *kophinos*) of food that were left after the feeding of the five thousand and the seven basketfuls (*spuris*) after the feeding of the four thousand. It's not difficult for God to provide for those who are obediently trusting him. The real problem is to get people to soften their hearts so they will recognize and embrace the new things God is doing in their midst. Jesus appears to get frustrated in this episode, but he's not necessarily frustrated at his disciples. He may simply be aware of how little time he has to prepare them for what's ahead and wonder what he has to do to make them understand.

> ⊃ Jesus expects his disciples to understand about God's power to provide because they've just witnessed two miraculous feedings. What lesson can God reasonably expect you to have learned through recent significant experiences that you've had? How can you take this lesson to heart so you don't have to relearn it before moving on to the next things God wants you to understand?

4 As he did when he healed the deaf man, Jesus uses saliva and the laying on of hands as extensions of himself to make a physical connection with the blind man. More significantly, Jesus takes both men away from the crowds. This is just what he's been doing with his disciples when he instructs them. The parallel shows that the two healings, in addition to being miracles that declare the coming of the kingdom of God, also symbolize the way the disciples, who "have eyes but fail to see, and ears but fail to hear," will eventually come to understand who Jesus is.

But this will happen in stages, just as the blind man initially sees people who look like trees walking around and then, after Jesus lays his hands on him again, he comes to see everything clearly. The first stage of understanding for the disciples comes when Peter declares that Jesus is the *Messiah*. This term hasn't been heard in Mark's gospel since the prologue; Peter is the first character in the main narrative to catch on to this much. But Peter is actually seeing a Messiah who looks like a tree walking around—the details are still fuzzy. In the second part of Mark, it will become much clearer what kind of Messiah Jesus actually is.

> ↪ Act III ends with this report of how the disciples responded to the question of Jesus' identity, just as Act I ended with a report of the Pharisees' response and Act II ended with a report of his family and neighbors' response. What people do you know today who are responding to Jesus in these same ways:
>
> I. Jesus represents such a dangerous and subversive influence that he has to be eliminated.
> II. Jesus is an ordinary human being whose words and acts have been blown out of proportion.
> III. Jesus is the Messiah or Savior, and I *think* I know what that means.
>
> How would you help each of these people understand better who Jesus is, based on your reading and study of the first part of Mark?

SESSION 13

JESUS PREDICTS HIS SUFFERINGS AND APPEARS IN GLORY ON A MOUNTAINTOP

Gospel of Mark > Part Two > Act IV: Journey to Jerusalem

INTRODUCTION

As the second part of Mark's gospel begins, Jesus takes his disciples on a long journey so he can explain to them *what kind of* Messiah he is. As we saw last time, the first part of the gospel culminates in Peter's declaration that Jesus is the Messiah. But even though Peter correctly identifies him, Jesus still warns the disciples not to tell anyone about him. They're not to proclaim *who* he is until they understand better *what* he is.

Peter makes his declaration at Caesarea Philippi. Of all the places that Jesus and his disciples visit in the gospel of Mark, this one is practically the northernmost. Over the course of Act IV, their journey will take them down to Jerusalem, the southernmost point they will reach. Almost every episode will feature a private conversation about the implications for Jesus' identity of events that transpire along the way. Mark begins Act IV by saying that Jesus "began to teach" his disciples. This phrase introduces the theme of the whole act, not just the first episode. Mark will later note that on this trip Jesus avoided the crowds "because he was teaching his disciples." The entire journey to Jerusalem is a walking classroom dedicated to the question of what it means for Jesus to be the Messiah.

READING

Read the first two episodes of Act IV out loud like a play, beginning with "He then began to teach them that the Son of Man must suffer many things" and ending with "Elijah has come, and they have done to him everything they wished, just as it is written about him." Have people take these parts:
- Narrator
- Jesus
- Peter
- Voice from the cloud
- Disciples (spokesperson)

When Mark says in the second episode that Jesus was "transfigured," this means that his face and probably his entire appearance were changed. This episode is often called the Transfiguration.

DISCUSSION

1 Peter has just identified Jesus as the Messiah. But in response, Jesus describes himself by a different term, the Son of Man. As we noted in session 4, this title highlights his humanity and humility. Jesus uses it to explain that to fulfill his Messianic mission, he must be rejected by the nation's elites, suffer and die, and then rise from the dead.

The disciples have trouble understanding what this last phrase means, and in any event, this whole sequence isn't what the Jewish people are expecting of their Messiah. To this point Jesus has done many of the things they are anticipating. He has healed the sick, brought liberation from demonic oppression and explained the meaning of the law with clarity and authority. All of this should culminate, according to popular expectations, in the nation uniting behind his leadership and driving the Roman occupiers out of their land. Instead, Jesus predicts, the people will turn against him and deliver him into the hands of the Romans as a troublemaker to be eliminated.

This is too much for Peter, who tries to set Jesus straight about how the Messiah's story is supposed to end. Jesus then explains to the disciples and everyone around them that he must personally take the path of suffering and sacrifice. Anyone who wants to be his true follower must take this path as well.

⊃ Jesus calls Peter "Satan" for trying to divert him from the path of suffering—this is how contrary Peter's notions are to the true values and methods of the kingdom of God. Jesus warns Peter similarly that he has "human concerns" in mind (that is, the preoccupations of this age, the "worries of this life") rather than the "concerns of God." What values and priorities of your own culture are most likely to divert a person from the path God has for them?

⊃ Jesus tells his potential followers that they each need to take up their own crosses. He's evoking a vivid figure from the experience of Roman occupation: condemned criminals carrying to the place of their own execution the crosses on which they will suffer horrible deaths. Sometimes we speak of things that merely try our patience as a "cross we have to bear." But Jesus is talking here about our being prepared literally to die, and at the very least to make sacrifices that effectively ruin our prospects in this world, in order to advance the kingdom of God. What examples can you give of people you know who've done this? How have they sacrificed and suffered, and how has this advanced God's kingdom?

2 Even though the kingdom of God advances through suffering and sacrifice, it's nevertheless an irresistibly powerful force that will inevitably reshape the world. For the moment, the kingdom is arriving in obscure ways and expanding largely unnoticed, as Jesus has explained in his parables. But it has nevertheless come with an inherent power that, Jesus promises, a fortunate few will glimpse even before its glorious culmination. This promise is fulfilled, at least in part, when Jesus takes his three renamed disciples—Peter, James and John—up a high mountain where he suddenly appears in dazzling brightness.

Jesus is joined on the mountain by two great figures from Israelite history, Elijah and Moses. Interpreters suggest many different things that their presence could signify (for example, that the Law and the Prophets, symbolized by Moses and Elijah, point to Jesus). But whatever else it means, their appearance helps clarify the identity of Jesus—the question that's foremost in the gospel of Mark at this point. Jesus isn't Elijah, not if the two of them are standing there together. And he also isn't the prophet who was going to come and be like Moses, not if he's being contrasted with Moses as well.

Then who is he? In almost the same language that Jesus heard at his baptism in the prologue, the voice from the cloud tells Peter, James and John, "This is my Son, whom I love." Here in the center of the gospel, characters in the main narrative hear for the first time that Jesus is the Son of God. And one of them has just declared, also for the first time in the narrative, that he is the Messiah. The meaning of the two titles Mark uses for Jesus at the very beginning of the gospel is beginning to be fleshed out. The disciples still don't understand everything. But they're at least starting to recognize what they need to understand, as their discussion on the way down the mountain of "rising from the dead" demonstrates.

> ⮕ Have you, or has someone you know, gotten a glimpse of the power and glory of the kingdom of God in this life, even though it usually arrives in quieter, humbler ways? If so, share with the group what happened.

> ⮕ What things about following Jesus do you recognize that you need to understand, even if you don't understand them yet?

> ⮕ Working individually, in teams, or as a group, retell the story of the Transfiguration from Peter's perspective. Speak in the first person, saying "I," "my," etc. How do you feel about Jesus, who called you "Satan" earlier in the week, as you walk up the mountain with him? What's your reaction to the change in his appearance and to the unexpected arrival of Elijah and Moses? Why do you suggest building shelters for them? Why do you address Jesus as "Rabbi," or teacher, under these circumstances? What do you think he means by "rising from the dead"? What makes you and the other two disciples ask more about Elijah? When you get back down the mountain, is it easy for you to obey

Jesus' orders not to tell anyone about this experience? Once you've written your version of the story from Peter's perspective, share it with your group or in a larger worship gathering. (You can also conduct an interview as you did in session 4 with a volunteer portraying Peter and answering these questions.)

SESSION 14

JESUS DELIVERS A BOY FROM A DEMON AND TEACHES HIS DISCIPLES PRIVATELY

Gospel of Mark > Part Two > Act IV: Journey to Jerusalem, continued

INTRODUCTION

As Jesus works his way down to Jerusalem with his disciples, he finds further opportunities to teach them what it means for him to be the Messiah and for them to follow him. The disciples' failure to cast out a demon provides the occasion for an important lesson about spiritual authority. After Jesus predicts his own sufferings a second time, an argument the disciples have about which one of them is the greatest prompts him to teach them about attitudes and relationships within the kingdom of God.

READING

Read these next episodes out loud like a play, beginning with "When they came to the other disciples, they saw a large crowd around them" and ending with "Have salt among yourselves, and be at peace with each other." Have people take these parts:
- Narrator
- Jesus
- Father of the boy with a demon

- Disciples (spokesperson)
- John

DISCUSSION

1 The account of the father who asks the disciples to drive a demon out of his son is much like other episodes in which Mark begins one story and then tells another before finishing the first. The problem of the disciples' inability to drive out the demon is raised at the beginning of the account and then addressed at the end, after Mark describes how Jesus was able to deliver the boy.

Jesus' explanation is puzzling at first. He says, "This kind can come out only by prayer," as if this were a particular kind of demon that called for specialized means of deliverance. However, even though Jesus doesn't pray here, he's able to deliver the boy anyway. And nowhere else does Jesus try to identify what kind of demon he's dealing with so he can employ the appropriate means; he simply commands and all demons obey. So Jesus' words more likely mean something else. "This kind" describes not this kind of *demon*, but this kind of *being*—that is, any type of demon. And by prayer, Jesus means that his disciples should cultivate a relationship of close dependence on God, so that what they do won't come from themselves, but from the power and authority of God that's flowing through them.

In other words, the spiritual authority to do things such as driving out demons must be either *direct, delegated* or *derived*. Jesus has *direct* spiritual authority because he is the Son of God—as terrified demons have frequently acknowledged. The disciples were able to drive out demons when Jesus sent them out earlier because he *delegated* his authority to them for that mission. But under any other circumstances, the disciples must *derive* their spiritual authority from God by cultivating a close relationship with him through prayer.

⮕ Do you feel that you've had experiences of using either delegated or derived spiritual authority? If so, describe them for the group. Do you see a connection between prayer and derived spiritual authority? Why or why not?

⊃ The disciples learned something earlier when their mission succeeded. Now they're invited to learn something else when they fail in an area where they previously succeeded. What are some of the most important lessons you've learned through both success and failure?

2 The contrast between faith and fear, which Mark drew so pointedly in Act II, emerges once again here in Act IV.

First, Jesus responds to the disciples' failure to cast out the demon by declaring their entire generation "unbelieving," or without faith. (Recall from session 8 that the English words "faith" and "believe" are translating the same Greek root.)

Next, the father of the boy has some faith, but he also struggles with a lack of faith and asks Jesus to help him with this. Apparently this is enough for Jesus to work with, since he casts out the demon.

Finally, when Jesus predicts his sufferings and death a second time, the disciples are afraid to ask him what this means. Instead of striving to understand what's happening in the kingdom so they can become involved with it, they take a step back out of fear.

⊃ The father's example suggests that faith and a lack of faith can coexist in a person whom God will help. How much faith do you think a person has to have in proportion to their lack of faith in order for God to work in their life? Consider the greatest spiritual challenge you're facing right now. What faith, and what lack of faith, are you bringing to it? If you prayed, as this father did, "Help me overcome my unbelief," what do you think God would do in answer to your prayer?

⊃ Jesus tells the father, "Everything is possible for one who believes." This statement is sometimes taken to mean that we can get God to do anything we want if we just believe hard enough. But in the context of these episodes, it actually means that when a person discerns that God is at work, nothing can stand in their way if they want to join in. Have you ever heard the statement interpreted the first way? If so, when and where? What were the results? If you understood the statement the second way, what area of your life would it most apply to right now? What would it encourage you to do?

3 John, one of the impetuous "sons of thunder," takes Jesus' lesson about spiritual authority too far. He tries to stop someone from driving out demons in Jesus' name because he's not part of their close circle. It's possible that John is feeling a sense of exclusive spiritual privilege after witnessing the Transfiguration. If Peter and James are feeling the same thing, this may explain why the disciples argue among themselves about which of them is the greatest. Jesus uses a little child to illustrate that humility, simplicity and service constitute true greatness in the kingdom of God.

John has correctly grasped that exorcisms aren't to be attempted on an individual's own authority. But he hasn't grasped something else. Since the person he tries to stop is performing exorcisms successfully, he can't be using Jesus' name just as a magic word. He must be identifying personally with Jesus and discerning God's purposes by faith. Anyone like this, Jesus insists, is on our side and shouldn't be opposed.

Indeed, Jesus says, hindering such a person might cause them to *stumble*. The term, as in Act II, is *scandalize*. If a person were operating in faith, but was still forbidden to identify with Jesus and his work, their moral sense would be rightly offended and they might unfortunately give up their activities. This observation leads Jesus to stress, in a series of compact pronouncements that make use of vivid metaphors and hyperbole (overstatement), that his followers should take any measures necessary to ensure that they're putting no stumbling blocks in the way of the kingdom.

➲ Jesus says, "Whoever is not against us is for us." Are there followers of Jesus that you may have been thinking of as opponents who, you can now recognize, are actually on the same team with you?

➲ The word that's translated "hell" in this passage is actually *Gehenna*, meaning the Valley of Hinnom just outside Jerusalem where garbage was dumped. There fires smoldered perpetually and worms worked through the refuse. In other words, these details aren't necessarily literal details of hell; Jesus is using this location as a metaphor for the isolation and disintegration that a person would experience if they turned definitively away from God. How do you picture the fate of such a person? What other images would you use to describe it?

☒ Jesus uses salt as an image in two senses: as a seasoning, to depict how difficult times can bring maturity ("salted with fire"), and as a preservative, to describe an attitude that makes for good relationships. If you wanted to create a modern-day parable, what objects or substances in your own culture could you use to represent these same effects?

SESSION 15

JESUS TEACHES HIS DISCIPLES MORE ABOUT THE WAYS OF THE KINGDOM OF GOD

Gospel of Mark > Part Two > Act IV: Journey to Jerusalem, continued

INTRODUCTION

Even though Jesus is trying to avoid the crowds so he can teach his disciples, it's hard for him to pass unnoticed as he reaches Judea, the southern part of the land of Palestine where Jerusalem is located. The Pharisees try to trap him once again, while parents ask him to bless their children and a would-be follower wants to know what he must do to obtain eternal life. All of these apparent interruptions provide further opportunities for Jesus to explain to his disciples the distinctive values of the kingdom of God.

READING

Read the next three episodes in Act IV out loud like a play, beginning with "Jesus then left that place and went into the region of Judea" and ending with "But many who are first will be last, and the last first." Have people take these parts:
- Narrator
- Pharisees
- Jesus

- Man who asks about eternal life
- Disciples
- Peter

DISCUSSION

1 The Pharisees try to trap Jesus by asking him about a controversial issue, divorce. Some rabbis taught that a man could divorce his wife for just about any reason, while others allowed it only for the most serious causes. No matter how Jesus answers, he'll contradict one group of teachers or another, and potentially offend much of the population. He could also put himself in even more danger with Herod if he suggests that his marriage to Herodias is invalid.

But Jesus takes a strong, clear stand on the issue. He sees this as another area in which the Pharisees and teachers of the law are setting aside the commands of God and replacing them with human traditions. In marriage, Jesus explains from the Scriptures, God makes the husband and wife one, so humans don't have the right or authority to make them two again by allowing divorce.

By referring to husband and wife in scriptural terms as "one flesh," Jesus is envisioning marriage as a relationship of unity and mutuality. This reflects the values of the kingdom Jesus has been teaching his disciples about, in which greatness consists of humility and service to others.

> ◌ Jesus says that Moses only permitted divorce because of the people's hardened hearts. As we noted in session 10, this expression describes people who have settled on a conclusion and aren't open to other possibilities. By contrast, do you know anyone whose marriage seemed doomed but who helped save the relationship by recognizing new possibilities for it or by seeing it in a new light? If so, share their story if you can. If you're personally in a troubled marriage, ask yourself whether you may have hardened your heart against your spouse or against God's ideal purposes for your relationship. Prayerfully consider whether

softening your heart and being open to previously unimagined possibilities could help you find renewed hope.

⊃ Should followers of Jesus take his response to the Pharisees here as the final word about divorce and remarriage and never permit these under any circumstances? If not, what complementary biblical principles can they use to help address difficult situations? Give examples, if you can, of complicated cases that you feel have been treated wisely and well.

2 The disciples try to discourage parents from bringing their children to Jesus because, like their society as a whole, they consider children unimportant. But Jesus believes just the opposite. "The kingdom of God belongs to such as these," he insists, and takes the children in his arms and blesses them.

⊃ When Jesus says it's necessary to receive the kingdom of God "like a little child," he's describing the simple, trusting, accepting way in which young children relate to other people. When have you seen a child do something adults might hesitate to do that reflected the values of the kingdom of God?

3 When a rich, lawkeeping man runs up to Jesus and expresses a keen interest in eternal life, the disciples are thinking, "Now here comes someone really important." Jesus is impressed too, at first. When he hears of the man's devotion and spiritual desire, he's filled with affection for this promising potential disciple. Jesus extends him a rare invitation to become part of the close circle around him. All the man has to do is leave his possessions behind as the other disciples have done. But this turns out to be a deal-breaker. The man has consistently made disciplined and sacrificial lifestyle choices in order to obey the commandments, but he won't part with his money. Anything but that. Jesus uses his case to describe how hard it is for rich people to enter the kingdom of God. The disciples are amazed, because they consider the rich to be objects of God's special favor and blessing. The experience is one more opportunity for them to discover that the values of God's kingdom are opposite to the values of this present age.

⊃ What kinds of people in your culture would be considered the best potential catches for the kingdom of God? (Some people regard the rich with resentment and suspicion; who would they see as especially favored instead?) Do you think it's a good strategy for a local community of Jesus' followers to give special priority to recruiting these "great catches"? Why or why not?

⊃ What is your "anything but"? Are you prepared to follow Jesus so long as it doesn't require one thing of you in particular? For example:
- going to live in a less-developed country
- being single
- raising your own support as a missionary, campus worker, etc.
- being imprisoned

If a person becomes aware that something like this is currently a deal-breaker for them, what can they do to keep it from preventing them from following Jesus wholeheartedly?

⊃ When Jesus says that anyone who leaves something for his sake will receive "a hundred times as much" in this life, this is likely a hyperbolic (overstated) way of saying that God will provide them with anything and everything they need to serve him. (We've seen this illustrated earlier in the gospel of Mark, for example, as the disciples who left their boats behind have somehow had the use of boats to transport Jesus on the lake.) Share with the group any experiences you've had of God providing something for you in a special way so that you could fulfill an important assignment.

SESSION 16

JESUS TEACHES ABOUT GREATNESS AND HEALS BLIND BARTIMAEUS

Gospel of Mark > Part Two > Act IV: Journey to Jerusalem, concluded

INTRODUCTION

Act IV has been about the disciples coming to understand who Jesus is. This was also the theme of Act III. By the end of that act, Peter was able to identify Jesus as the Messiah. As the disciples have now traveled the length of the country with Jesus, they've learned much more about what kind of Messiah he is. But even as they close in on their ultimate destination of Jerusalem, there are still some important lessons that must be underscored, as an inappropriate request by James and John shows.

The two acts in the middle of the gospel of Mark (Acts III and IV) both end with the healing of a blind man. At the end of Act III this takes place in two stages, illustrating that the disciples have come to a partial understanding that still needs to be sharpened. In the final scene of Act IV a man named Bartimaeus receives his sight all at once. This signifies that the disciples have finally learned enough that they should be able to understand the meaning and implications of Jesus' sufferings when they take place shortly in Jerusalem, as he has repeatedly predicted.

READING

Read the concluding episodes of Act IV out loud like a play, beginning with "They were on their way up to Jerusalem, with Jesus leading the way" and ending with "Immediately he received his sight and followed Jesus along the road." Have people take these parts:

- Narrator
- Jesus
- James and John
- Bartimaeus
- People in the crowd

DISCUSSION

1 Jesus has predicted his sufferings, death and resurrection three times in Act IV. Each time, one of his three closest disciples has responded by contradicting him, explicitly or implicitly, and he has had to correct them for the benefit of the whole group:

Peter rebukes Jesus after the first prediction, and Jesus has to counter, "Get behind me, Satan! You do not have in mind the concerns of God, but merely human concerns."

After the second prediction, John announces that he has tried to stop someone outside their group from driving out demons in Jesus' name. Jesus has to explain that whoever isn't against them is for them.

Now, after the third prediction, James and John ask to sit at the right and left hand of Jesus in his glory. This provides the occasion for another corrective teaching.

The two brothers may feel a sense of privilege because Jesus has given them exclusive access to important scenes like the Transfiguration and the raising of Jairus's daughter. They may think this means Jesus also wants them to have privileged positions in the kingdom of God, as they're envisioning it. Jesus informs them, "You don't know what you are asking." If they really want to be by Jesus' side, this will require suffering with him. (Drinking a cup is an image from the Hebrew Scriptures for undergoing an experience of suffering; baptism is used here not as a sign of cleansing from sin but rather as a figure for being immersed in a flood of troubles.)

And even though James and John will endure suffering faithfully for Jesus' sake (this prediction is meant to encourage them), they can't expect special rewards for this. Any privileges in the kingdom will be distributed as God sees fit.

> ⮕ What kinds of things might a person pray for today that would lead Jesus to respond, "You don't know what you are asking"? What would the person who made this request need to understand better?

> ⮕ Suppose that there are places of honor in the kingdom of God and that they belong to those who are the greatest because they are the least and the servants of all. What people or kinds of people do you picture being given these places?

2 Bartimaeus must have already heard about Jesus as a teacher and healer, and he must have come to believe that he is the Messiah, because he addresses him loudly with a Messianic title, Son of David. (By contrast, the people who tell Bartimaeus of his approach describe him simply as Jesus of Nazareth.) But it's not yet clear what kind of Messiah Bartimaeus believes Jesus to be. He's a beggar, and his request, "Have mercy on me," could simply be a way of asking for money, perhaps as a grand gesture on the part of an ambitious leader intent on reclaiming the throne of David. So Jesus gets him to be more specific: "What do you want me to do for you?" When Bartimaeus says he wants to receive his sight, Jesus recognizes that he's asking in bold faith for something that will help declare the coming of the kingdom of God. He tells him, as he did the woman who suffered from bleeding, "Your faith has healed you."

Bartimaeus has discerned the activity of God behind the ministry of Jesus, and in confident expectation he has taken bold initiative. Mark recounts his healing at this point in the gospel as a symbolic illustration of the progress the disciples should be making in understanding who Jesus is. But Bartimaeus himself is also one of several characters in the story who grasps Jesus' identity by faith and whose life is radically transformed as a result.

➲ Relive this story from the perspective of Bartimaeus by having a volunteer portray him and having another group member interview him and ask questions like these: Why were you begging just outside Jericho on the road to Jerusalem the day Jesus passed by? How had you heard about him? How did you decide among the many different opinions people had about him? Why did you keep shouting when the crowd told you to be quiet? What was it like when Jesus called you to himself? What gave you the boldness to ask for your sight instead of for something else? When Jesus said you could go, why did you decide to follow him along the road? How far did you follow him, and what did you see? The person who portrays Bartimaeus should use their imagination and responsible speculation to fill in any details necessary to tell a complete story. (You can also write up a story in the first person, as you did in session 13.)

➲ In each of these last two episodes in Act IV, Jesus asks someone, "What do you want me to do for you?" James and John ask for something inappropriate that's contrary to the purposes of the kingdom of God; Bartimaeus asks in bold faith for something that will advance the kingdom. How would you respond if Jesus asked you, "What do you want me to do for you?" (Think carefully!)

SESSION 17

JESUS ENTERS JERUSALEM, MAKES A FIG TREE WITHER, AND CLEANSES THE TEMPLE

Gospel of Mark > Part Two > Act V: Confrontation in Jerusalem

INTRODUCTION

To this point Jesus has guarded his identity carefully. He's explained the kingdom of God mostly to his disciples and ordered the few people who've realized who he is not to tell anyone. But now, as he reaches Jerusalem, he changes his approach dramatically. He enters the city in a way that boldly stakes his claim to be the Messiah. He then asserts his authority over the activities in the temple courts. As he does these things, he quotes and alludes to the Hebrew Scriptures, implying that he is the fulfillment of their predictions. All of this will bring him into conflict with the nation's civic and religious leadership. But this is precisely what he has in mind. Their resistance will provide him with the opportunity, over the course of Act V, to explain the true nature of the kingdom of God to the crowds from all over the country that are gathering in the city.

READING

Read the first two episodes of Act V out loud like a play, beginning with "As they approached Jerusalem and came to Bethphage and Bethany at the

Mount of Olives" and ending with "forgive them, so that your Father in heaven may forgive you your sins."

Have people take these parts:
- Narrator
- Jesus
- People in the street
- People in the crowd
- Peter

DISCUSSION

1 Jesus and his disciples have come to Jerusalem for the festival of Passover. It was customary to travel to this festival on foot, and that's how they've come most of the distance. But now, for the first and only time in the gospel, Jesus rides as an equestrian into the city. This was how a victorious general would return in triumph or a new king would arrive for coronation. Looming above the crowds on foot, he's making an intentionally dramatic impression. But Jesus has specifically chosen a colt (young donkey) as his mount, not a war horse or magnificent stallion. The choice of this humble animal shows that he comes in peace, as a different kind of king. It also alludes to Zechariah's prophecy that Jerusalem's promised king would arrive "lowly and riding on a donkey."

The crowds get much of the message, and in response, they too echo the Scriptures, shouting greetings to Jesus in the words of Psalm 118. This psalm was written to welcome pilgrims into the temple, but the crowds give it a Messianic twist. When they address Jesus as one who "comes in the name of the Lord," they're turning this phrase into an implicit Messianic title. This is clear from the way they add a further phrase: "Blessed is the coming kingdom of our father David!" As far as they're concerned, Jesus is the long-expected Son of David, come to liberate the nation. Later, as Jesus teaches in the temple, he will challenge the people's understanding of what it means for him to be the Son of David. But this is good enough for a start.

➲ The success of Jesus' plan to enter Jerusalem in this symbolic way hinges on the cooperation of the colt's owner, who isn't identified, but who seems to have made the animal available to Jesus upon request. He has apparently left instructions with his family and servants to let anyone take the colt who uses the agreed-upon phrase "The Lord needs it." What resources can you put at God's disposal, to be called upon as needed? Agree with God on a sign or a phrase that will show he's taking you up on your offer, and see what happens.

➲ Jesus leads the crowds to draw a conclusion about himself that's on the right track, but not entirely correct. Is this the best that can be expected of them at this point? Has God shown you some things in stages? If so, describe for the group how your understanding of one truth about God has grown and been clarified.

2 We've often seen Mark tell one story in the middle of another for suspense and dramatic effect. But now he takes this technique to the next level. He weaves the stories of Jesus cleansing the temple and withering the fig tree so tightly together that we understand each one in light of the other. The fig tree, in full leaf in the spring as if it were the summer fruit-bearing season, is all show and no fruit—just like the temple, which is bustling with activity but actually devoted to commerce instead of prayer and worship. The tree's deceptive appearance mirrors what Jesus observed in the temple courts the evening before, and he announces the same judgment against the tree that he will shortly proclaim against the temple: destruction.

But the temple won't be destroyed immediately; it still has a purpose to serve, as a gathering place for the people to hear Jesus answer the questions and challenges of the nation's leaders. So, alluding to more prophecies by Isaiah ("a house of prayer for all nations") and Jeremiah ("a den of robbers"), Jesus drives out the merchants so the temple courts can serve as the setting for these sharp and illuminating exchanges.

➲ Do your external activities give an accurate impression of the amount of spiritual life you have inside you? In other words, what's your current fruit-to-leaf ratio?

➲ The fig tree serves as a kind of parable, an important object lesson, but in this case it's a real-life one. Its owner suffers a significant financial loss when it withers beyond recovery. Is it justifiable for Jesus to use someone else's tree in this way? (Is this another case of "the Lord needs it"?)

➲ Changing money and selling doves were necessary for the ongoing operation of the temple. Only coins without human images could be used inside the temple precincts, and doves were an affordable kind of sacrifice. But these commercial activities had now overtaken the temple area to such an extent that prayer and worship were being crowded out. If you're part of a community of Jesus' followers, share with the group how it handles the necessary commercial side of its existence and what measures it takes to keep this from crowding out spiritual activities.

3 Even though Jesus is setting the stage for his public teaching in the temple, these interwoven stories end with one more episode of Jesus instructing his disciples privately. The temple has become a "den of robbers," so the community of Jesus' followers must become the new "house of prayer." Significantly, Jesus' instructions here are in the plural: Have faith in God (all of you); whatever you (together) ask for in prayer, believe (all of you) that you have received it; and so forth. It's not up to individuals to decide what they want and then believe hard enough to make it happen. Individual ideas, wishes, and desires are to be tested by the community's corporate discernment so that its members can pray together with bold confidence for what will further God's purposes.

➲ Have you had an experience where you worked with others to discern how you should pray for something and were then able to pray for it with bolder faith? If so, tell the group about it.

➲ If you're part of a community of Jesus' followers, in what ways is it currently a "house of prayer"? In what ways would you like to see it become a house of prayer even more?

SESSION 18

THE JEWISH LEADERS QUESTION JESUS' AUTHORITY AND IDENTITY

Gospel of Mark > Part Two > Act V: Confrontation in Jerusalem, continued

INTRODUCTION

As Jesus expected and intended, his actions provoke a confrontation with the nation's civic and religious leaders. The Sanhedrin, the ruling political body made up of chief priests, teachers of the law, and elders, sends a delegation to question him. They demand to know by whose authority he has taken charge of the temple courts. (They want to make it clear that they haven't given him their permission!)

The question of Jesus' authority implicitly raises the question of his identity: *Who does he think he is* to act like this? Jesus doesn't answer their question directly. But through a counter-question and a parable, he reveals his identity to anyone in the crowd who has eyes to see and ears to hear.

READING

Read these next two episodes of Act V out loud like a play, beginning with "They arrived again in Jerusalem" and ending with "But they were afraid of the crowd; so they left him and went away." Have people take these parts:

- Narrator
- Sanhedrin delegation
- Jesus

DISCUSSION

1 When the Sanhedrin delegation challenges Jesus' authority, he seems to have only two options. He can make the outrageous claim that he's been sent directly by God, or the embarrassing admission that he's been acting only on his own initiative. Either reply, his opponents are confident, will discredit him with the crowds.

But Jesus instead answers with a question of his own. (This was an accepted way to respond in exchanges like this. Earlier, when the Pharisees questioned him about divorce, he countered, "What did Moses command you?") Jesus asks the delegation about John the Baptist. John, like Jesus, did something that required spiritual authority—he baptized people and declared that their sins were forgiven. But John, like Jesus, was never given any authority by the Sanhedrin. So was he just acting on his own initiative, or was he genuinely sent by God?

We learn here for the first time that the members of the Sanhedrin were not among "all the people of Jerusalem" who went out to hear John. They didn't believe his message. So they're not about to say that his authority came from God. But they don't dare say he was simply acting on his own. So they declare the source of John's authority to be an open question. This is good enough for Jesus, who says he'll let the same conclusion apply to his own authority. This allows him to continue operating freely for the time being.

The exchange suggests several important things about Jesus' identity. At the beginning and end of Act III the question was raised whether Jesus might be John the Baptist. No, we see here, they're two different people, since the authority of each can be considered separately. But since John is someone whose authority cannot be publicly questioned, his prediction should be taken seriously that someone greater would follow him—a Messianic figure who would baptize with the Holy Spirit. Since Jesus has the same kind of authority as John, perhaps he is this greater successor.

⊃ Have you ever heard someone answer a hostile question with another question that effectively neutralized the opposition? (Have you done this yourself?) If so, tell the group what happened.

⊃ As a group, list the kinds of activities that you believe require spiritual authority. (For example, baptizing someone, leading an observance of the Lord's Supper, preaching in church, assuring someone that their sins are forgiven, etc.) What would give you the confidence that a person had the spiritual authority to do these things?

2 Jesus' parable is so reminiscent of a similar story by the prophet Isaiah that none of his listeners should have any difficulty understanding who the characters represent. (Indeed, the members of the Sanhedrin recognize immediately that he's telling the parable against them.) The vineyard owner represents God; the tenants represent the people of Israel, and especially their leaders; the servants represent the prophets. The son represents Jesus himself. This character's death is the climax of the story, and Jesus' own opponents are looking for a way to kill him.

In addition to discrediting the nation's leaders as disobedient and resistant to God, the parable sheds further light on Jesus' identity. The question was also raised earlier in the book whether he was one of the prophets. No, since he's not depicted as a servant like them. Instead, he's described as the beloved son of the vineyard owner. Mark's readers have an advantage that most of Jesus' listeners don't. They've heard Jesus described as God's beloved Son at his baptism and during the Transfiguration. Even so, the most discerning in the crowd will recognize that Jesus is identifying himself through this story as the Son of God.

The parable of the vineyard is a fourth prediction by Jesus of his sufferings, death, and resurrection. (The parable ends with the son dead, but Jesus then quotes from Psalm 118, describing a surprising reversal in which a stone that was originally rejected is elevated to a position of honor. This symbolically depicts his resurrection.) Jesus told his disciples earlier that he would give his life "as a ransom for many," and in the parable the son's death causes possession of the vineyard to be transferred to "others." This foreshadows the acceptance of Gentiles like Mark's Roman audience as part of the people of God.

> ◌ Jesus' parables often have a certain shock value that's intended to provoke deeper reflection. In this case the shock isn't that tenant farmers would try to avoid giving a share of their crop to an absentee landlord. Instead, it's that the landlord keeps sending servant after servant to them, and then his only son, long after the tenants have demonstrated that they'll injure or kill anyone who tries to collect the crop. The landlord's patience and trust in the tenants' sense of responsibility seem naive at best and dangerously misguided at worst. Is this an accurate portrayal of God? Or would God act against this kind of hardened resistance much sooner?

> ◌ The real-life parable of the fig tree has the same message as this spoken parable: When fruit is to be expected, but none is forthcoming, there will be judgment. The fig tree, however, is destroyed immediately. Is this a more accurate portrayal of God than the one in the parable? Or are both portrayals exaggerated to make a point? How much patience and mercy can we expect from God?

> ◌ The father in the parable sends his son in the expectation that he will be treated respectfully and obeyed. But God the Father sent Jesus into the world knowing that he would be mistreated and killed. How could he do this?

SESSION 19

JESUS DEBATES HIS OPPONENTS AND TEACHES THE CROWDS IN THE TEMPLE

Gospel of Mark > Part Two > Act V: Confrontation in Jerusalem, continued

INTRODUCTION

The confrontation in the temple between Jesus and the nation's leaders continues for the rest of the week leading up to Passover. Mark doesn't describe the events of the entire week; instead, he relates significant episodes. Jesus' opponents continue to ask him difficult questions, hoping he will discredit himself or antagonize many of the people. But Jesus answers their questions so well that he's able to use his time in the temple to teach the gathered crowds more about the ways of the kingdom of God and his own identity. Even one of the teachers of the law is won over.

READING

Have group members take turns reading the episodes Mark relates from Jesus' time in the temple:
- The Pharisees and Herodians question Jesus.
- The Sadducees question Jesus.
- A teacher of the law questions Jesus.
- Jesus questions the people about the Messiah.

- Jesus warns the people about the teachers of the law.
- Jesus praises the generosity of a poor widow.

DISCUSSION

1 As an imposition by Rome on its conquered subjects, the imperial tax was naturally unpopular. But many Jews had a deeper objection to it. Historically their nation had been a theocracy, governed by kings and priests who were representatives of their own God. So acknowledging Caesar as their ruler through the payment of taxes felt like serving a false god. (A significant tax revolt had taken place some years earlier against serving "mortal masters in place of God.") The Pharisees and Herodians have created a dangerous trap. If Jesus says the people shouldn't pay the tax, he'll get in trouble with the Romans. But if he says they should pay, he's not just a collaborator, to many he's almost a blasphemer.

Jesus escapes the trap by challenging the assumption implicit in the question. He tacitly argues that a government doesn't have to be a theocracy. In this way he breaks free from the rigid framework his opponents have created out of the way God worked at one particular time in Israel's history. No matter what form of government God's people on earth happen to be living under, they can always give him their loyalty, devotion and gifts. Paying taxes to Caesar doesn't impinge on this. In fact, since they're the beneficiaries of the services the Roman Empire provides, they should do their share to provide for them. God is God, and Caesar has an empire to run. Next question.

> ➲ Would you rather live in (1) a society that sought to base its laws on the Bible and whose leaders had to meet a test of Christian faith or (2) a society that tried to preserve basic freedoms and whose laws and leaders were determined by the will of the people? Explain your answer.

> ➲ According to Jesus, the government has a legitimate claim to a certain portion of our resources, and so does God. The government's share is determined by our tax bracket. How can we

determine what God's share is, and how we're supposed to give it back to him?

2 The Sadducees' question also creates a trap. If Jesus denies the resurrection, he'll offend many of the people, including powerful groups like the Pharisees. But if he tries to establish which of the seven brothers the woman will be married to in the resurrection, he can't avoid looking foolish.

Like the previous question, this one is also posed within a rigid framework that's based exclusively on God's work at one particular time. The Sadducees believe only what is written in the "Book of Moses" (that is, the Torah, Genesis through Deuteronomy), not what's in the later Scriptures. And since they can't find any description of the resurrection in the Torah, they don't believe in it.

Jesus responds by appealing more broadly to "the Scriptures" as a whole to argue that since there's no marriage in the resurrection, the woman won't be married to any of the brothers. It's not clear what particular Scriptures Jesus has in mind as the basis for his argument, but he is drawing on a comprehensive understanding of God's ways to show that the Sadducees' question is based on a false premise: They think the next life will be pretty much like this one. As a finishing touch, Jesus demonstrates that there's evidence for the resurrection even in the Torah. God would never identify himself by people who, now dead and gone, knew him and served him only in the past. A living God is worshipped by living people. So if God is the God of the patriarchs, they must still be alive as well.

> ⭢ Jesus says that in the resurrection, people will be like the angels in heaven. What do you think will this look like, besides people not marrying?

> ⭢ How much of the Scriptures do you depend on for authoritative instruction about what you should believe and how you should live?
>
> > **a.** Only a certain part (for example, Paul's letters), on theological grounds

b. Only certain parts, effectively, because they're the only ones I read
   c. The New Testament, as the interpretive key to the whole
   d. All of the Bible, as the record of God's dealings with humanity throughout history
   e. The written Scriptures and the teachings that have flowed from them as they've since been interpreted and applied

3 One of the teachers of the law, who may have come to the temple originally to oppose Jesus, is so impressed by his reply to the Sadducees that he asks a sincere question and applauds Jesus' answer. This leads Jesus to assure him, "You are not far from the kingdom of God." This teacher has grasped that the kingdom is not about external observances, but about heartfelt devotion and loving actions.

➲ In what ways do you love God with each of the faculties Jesus mentions: your heart, soul, mind and strength? With which of these would you like to love God more?

➲ The exchange between Jesus and this teacher of the law seems to allow for a faith based on an ethic of love that dispenses with ritual observances. What continuing value do religious practices have for followers of Jesus?

➲ If this teacher of the law was "not far" from the kingdom of God, what more did he need to do to become part of it? Where would you put yourself: distant from the kingdom, not far from it, just inside or deeply involved?

4 To this point Jesus has accepted the Messianic title Son of David from people like Bartimaeus and the crowds entering Jerusalem. But now, as his opponents in the temple go silent, he uses the opportunity to challenge the people's understanding of how he actually relates to David. He quotes from Psalm 110 to argue that David recognized the future Messiah as his divine Lord, not merely his human descendant and royal successor. If Jesus truly is the Son of David or Messiah, then this means much more than the people have understood to this point. They're pleased and intrigued as they listen to him now. But Jesus' claims to be not just the Messiah, but also divine, will eventually cause the leaders and the crowds to clamor for his death.

Mark concludes his description of Jesus' time in the temple with two brief episodes that contrast the pretensions and greed of the teachers of the law with the sincere devotion of a poor widow. The contrast once again highlights the values of the kingdom of God, in which the quality of a gift matters far more than its quantity, and showy but easily affordable displays count far less than small but significant sacrifices.

> ⇒ What are the equivalents in your culture of the religious privileges and accolades the teachers of the law desired, and of the greed and false piety they displayed?

> ⇒ Think of a way you could give God a gift of high quality, no matter what its monetary value, and offer that gift sometime in the days ahead.

SESSION 20

JESUS PREDICTS THE DESTRUCTION OF THE TEMPLE

Gospel of Mark > Part Two > Act V: Confrontation in Jerusalem, concluded

INTRODUCTION

So far in Jerusalem, Jesus has reduced the nation's pretentious religious teachers to silence and exposed their pride and greed. Now he moves against the temple itself. He walks out of the building and sits opposite it. Within the narrative flow and thematic development of Mark's gospel, we can tell that Jesus isn't just on his way home for the day; he's dramatizing his rejection and condemnation of what the nation's religious life, embodied in the temple, has become. He declares openly that the temple will be reduced to rubble.

As they've often done before, some of Jesus' disciples come to him privately to request an explanation. They ask specifically when the temple will be destroyed and how they can know this is about to happen. Mark presents Jesus' reply at considerable length, so that the second part of the gospel (Acts IV–VI), like the first part (Acts I–III), has a concentrated block of his teaching near its center.

Certain aspects of Jesus' reply to the disciples seem straightforward. In answer to their question about when the temple will be destroyed, he explains that this will happen within the current generation: Some of the people then living will still be alive to see it. But other aspects of his reply are harder to understand. In response to the disciples' question about how they can recognize when the temple is about to be destroyed, he tells them somewhat cryptically to flee from Judea when they see "the abomination that causes desolation." Mark addresses his audience at this point ("let the reader understand") to explain that they need to reflect on this saying to appreciate its meaning and its implications for everything Jesus says in this discourse.

READING

Have group members take turns reading one paragraph at a time through this episode, beginning with "As Jesus was leaving the temple" and ending with "What I say to you, I say to everyone: 'Watch!'"

DISCUSSION

1 Many people today scrutinize Jesus' words here for clues about when and how the world is going to end. This is truly ironic, since Jesus' first concern is to dampen down this kind of speculation. He warns his disciples against the seductive appeal of "false messiahs and false prophets" who lead many people astray by their predictions. He cautions against reading heightened significance into disturbing but recurring historical events such as wars, earthquakes and famines. He insists that even he doesn't know the exact day and hour. Jesus tells his disciples repeatedly to be on their guard: The people who will be the least prepared for the future are those who are the most gullible.

> ➲ What examples can you give of people who have won a following by predicting the end of the world? What happened to their followers in the end?

> ➲ What makes people so susceptible to being captivated by end-of-the-world scenarios? How can a person be properly cautious about them, as Jesus commands?

2 Jesus explains that before the temple is destroyed, "the gospel must first be preached to all nations." This is because the Jewish temple is going to be replaced by a multinational community of Jesus' followers as the focal point of God's engagement with humanity. Such a community must be called into being for this to happen. Its creation will not be the sign that the temple is about to be destroyed, but it is a precondition for the momentous events Jesus is predicting.

And so the time between Jesus' words and their fulfillment must be a time of proclamation to all nations. It will also be a time of persecution and betrayal for Jesus' followers, but even these things will create opportunities for them to share the gospel at the highest levels of their societies, as the Holy Spirit inspires their words. And so, in addition to caution, the disciples must engage the days ahead with boldness, endurance, and trust.

➲ Do you know anyone who has endured the kind of persecution and betrayal Jesus describes here in order to bring the gospel to their family, friends and nation, or to another nation? If so, tell the group about them. In your prayer time, ask God to help each person mentioned to endure faithfully. Pray that they will see Jesus' promise fulfilled and receive the right words to speak just as they need them.

➲ Jesus concludes his discourse with a parable in which a householder gives each of his servants the responsibility and authority to fulfill their "assigned task" until he returns. What is your "assigned task" from God? How are you fulfilling it?

3 Interpreters are widely agreed that Jesus' prediction was fulfilled when the Jerusalem temple was destroyed in AD 70 at the end of the Jewish-Roman War. But they disagree about whether a further fulfillment of this prediction should also be expected in the future. The main reason for the disagreement is that interpreters understand differently the two references Jesus makes to the book of Daniel.

The first reference comes when Jesus names the specific sign that will indicate the temple is about to be destroyed. He refers to an "abomination that causes desolation standing where it does not belong." This phrase comes from a prophecy of Daniel that was fulfilled, at least initially, in 167 BC when a pagan emperor desecrated the Jerusalem temple by installing a statue of Zeus atop one of its altars. (This act led to the Maccabean revolt, during which the Jews recaptured, purified and rededicated the temple, a victory still celebrated each year in the festival of Hanukkah.) Jesus alludes to this passage to explain to his disciples that the warning sign of the temple's imminent destruction will be *something like* this sacrilege that occurred two centuries earlier. Mark adds a cautionary note to his readers not to expect it to be *exactly* the same.

Interpreters differ as to what this sign actually was when Jesus' prediction was fulfilled, but it provided evidence in some way that the temple would soon fall into the hands of hostile armies. Jesus warned that this would be a time of terrible distress for everyone living in Judea and that the only safe recourse would be to flee. Heeding his words, his followers did flee from Judea during the Jewish-Roman War.

These historical events would appear to account for everything Jesus says to this point. But he goes on to speak of a time "following that distress" when the sun, moon and stars will be darkened and "people will see the Son of Man coming in clouds with great power and glory." This is another allusion to Daniel, to his vision of "one like a son of man" coming with the clouds of heaven to receive "authority, glory and sovereign power" from God. (This vision was noted in session 4 as the source of Jesus' preferred title Son of Man.) The difference in interpreters' overall understandings of this discourse comes from their divergent beliefs about what this second allusion means.

Many interpreters believe that Jesus is describing his own return at the end of the world. For them, the description of the elect being gathered from the four winds is a reference to true believers being caught up to meet Jesus upon his return. These interpreters argue that Jesus is looking ahead through the events of AD 70 to the culmination of history and that this is actually the main thing he wants to describe. If this is the case, then the "generation" of people he mentions comes much later. The temple will be rebuilt in Jerusalem at some point, they will see it desecrated by a future abomination, and they will witness the final events of human history.

Other interpreters argue that Jesus' reference to Daniel's vision of the Son of Man should be understood the same way as his allusion to the "abomination that causes desolation"—symbolically, not literally. Understood this way, it describes Jesus receiving authority to rule over the kingdom of God that will eventually displace the kingdoms of the earth. In this interpretation, the extinction of the sun, moon and stars represents the overthrow and replacement of earthly powers (a meaning this symbol can have in the prophets). The gathering of the elect refers to the creation of a community of Jesus' followers from every nation.

> ➲ Let each member of the group state briefly, if they wish, what they think is the best way to understand what Jesus is predicting here, and why. In practical terms, what's at stake in the choice between interpretations for the way followers of Jesus understand their present-day responsibilities?

> ➲ To appreciate the impact that Jesus' words would have had on the disciples, picture him visiting your country, touring the most important public monuments in your capital, then walking out of them and declaring that they'll be reduced to rubble in your lifetime. If you believe Jesus when he says this, how does it affect the way you think about your country and your relationship to it?

FOR YOUR NEXT MEETING

You'll be invited to conclude the next session by sharing the Lord's Supper together as a group, if this is acceptable within your community. Arrange for this ahead of time by having bread and wine or grape juice available and deciding who will lead the observance and how you'd like the bread and the cup to be shared.

SESSION 21

JESUS SHARES A MEAL IN BETHANY AND OBSERVES PASSOVER IN JERUSALEM

Gospel of Mark > Part Two > Act VI: Jesus' Sufferings, Death, and Resurrection

INTRODUCTION

At the end of Act IV Jesus made his most detailed prediction of what would happen to him in Jerusalem. He told his disciples he would be delivered to the chief priests and teachers of the law, who would condemn him to death. They would hand him over to the Romans, who would mock him, spit on him, flog him and kill him. But on the third day he would rise from the dead. In Act VI of his gospel, Mark describes how each of these things happened just as Jesus predicted.

But Jesus also explained the purpose of his sufferings. He said that he would "give his life as a ransom for many," meaning that through his death others would be set free and given life. As Mark relates the final events of Jesus' life on earth, he shows how they fulfilled this purpose.

Act VI begins with two dinners. Jesus and his disciples have been staying in Bethany, a village just outside Jerusalem. But observant Jews were required to eat the Passover meal within the city. So as the festival approaches, they have a final meal with their friends in Bethany and then relocate to Jerusalem, where they celebrate Passover itself the next evening.[1]

---

[1] "Two days away," literally "after two days," means "the next day" in the gospel of Mark, where today is considered the first day and tomorrow the second day.

READING

Read the beginning of Act VI out loud like a play, beginning with "Now the Passover and the Festival of Unleavened Bread were only two days away" and ending with "But Peter insisted emphatically, 'Even if I have to die with you, I will never disown you.' And all the others said the same." Have people take these parts:

- Narrator
- Chief priests
- Simon's dinner guests
- Jesus
- Disciples
- Peter

DISCUSSION

1 The gospel of Mark only tells us about Jesus' ministry in Galilee, so other than the name of his host in Bethany, we don't know who he's having dinner with on the night before Passover or how he got to know these people. But clearly he's among friends who want to share this time with him before he and his disciples have to go into the city. One follower in particular expresses her love and devotion through an extravagant gesture. In this culture, pouring olive oil on someone's head was a customary way of showing welcome and honor. (It was also refreshing in the hot and dusty climate.) But this woman uses a jar of the most expensive perfume instead of olive oil, prompting protests and harsh criticism from the other guests. Jesus defends her, arguing that she has recognized the solemnity of the occasion and signified the deeper purpose of his impending trip into the city.

When Jesus says "the poor you will always have with you," he isn't excusing institutional poverty that's created by unjust economic relations. (He has just criticized the teachers of the law for exploiting the weak.) Rather, he's referring to people who become poor after suffering misfortunes, such as widows and orphans. Jesus adds that "you can help them any time you want." He expects his followers to be helping the poor regularly; he simply observes that acts of extravagant devotion on appropriate occasions don't have to conflict with this.

⊃ What is the monetary value of a year's wages in your society? Can you name a perfume or other luxury item that's worth this much? What would it look like for someone to expend this item quickly and publicly as an expression of devotion to Jesus? How would you react if someone did this? Is there any occasion that would make this appropriate, as Jesus' looming death did for the woman's lavish gesture?

⊃ In what ways do you help the poor? As a group, identify something you can do together to help those in need around you.

2 While Jesus is among friends in Bethany, he's being shadowed by enemies in Jerusalem. They find their opportunity to arrest him away from the crowds when Judas agrees to betray him. The danger is coming so close that Jesus warns his disciples at their Passover meal that he'll soon be taken and they'll all *fall away*. (Literally they will be *scandalized*, like the people represented by the second kind of soil in Jesus' earlier parable.)

Peter continues to feel superior to the others: "Even if all fall away," he insists, "I will not." He's suggesting that the other disciples can't be expected to show his degree of loyalty, since they haven't seen all the things he has. Peter thinks he will never disown Jesus, but Jesus counters that he'll do this within a day—in fact, before the night is even over, before the rooster crows twice.[2]

Jesus' parable of the householder showed how a night was divided into different parts: "in the evening, or at midnight, or when the rooster crows, or at dawn." Peter's bold resolution isn't even going to last until daybreak.

⊃ Mark doesn't explain why Judas agreed to betray Jesus; he leaves this to our imagination. Have one or more volunteers re-

---

[2] The other gospels have the rooster crowing only once. The best explanation may be that Mark, drawing on Peter's recollections, is reporting the story in more detail, while the other gospel writers are relating a simpler version that still brings out the main idea.

create out loud what they think was going on in Judas's head as he talked himself into betraying Jesus.

◌ In the company of Jesus and surrounded by friends, Peter couldn't imagine the enormous pressure he'd feel when he was isolated and threatened by the hostility of opponents and the power of the state. How can sincere followers of Jesus better anticipate this kind of pressure so they can remain loyal to him even if they experience it?

3 The festival of Passover commemorated the way God delivered the people of Israel from slavery in Egypt and established a covenant or special relationship with them. Jesus uses the occasion to announce that God is now making another covenant through his own sacrificial death. As we've noted, the two miraculous feedings earlier in the gospel foreshadow this Last Supper that Jesus shares with his disciples. (The language is intentionally similar: At all three events, Jesus takes bread, blesses it, breaks it and gives it to his disciples.) Since the feedings signified that the blessings of God are for both Jews and Gentiles, readers of Mark's gospel are meant to understand that the covenant in Jesus' blood will create a new people of God out of men and women from every nation.

◌ Ever since this night, followers of Jesus have reenacted what he did with the bread and the cup as a means of expressing their faith in the effects of his death. This ceremony has become known as the Lord's Supper, or Eucharist. If you're part of a community of Jesus' followers, share with the group how you celebrate the Lord's Supper. What's the most meaningful part of this ceremony for you, either as you observe it now, or as you've done so in the past?

◌ Conclude this session by sharing the Lord's Supper together as a group, if your members would like to and this is acceptable within your community.

SESSION 22

JESUS PRAYS IN GETHSEMANE AND IS ARRESTED AND QUESTIONED BY THE SANHEDRIN

Gospel of Mark > Part Two > Act VI: Jesus' Sufferings, Death, and Resurrection, continued

INTRODUCTION

Knowing that the terrible events he has predicted are just about to unfold, Jesus goes to a quiet place for a time of concentrated prayer and there he wrestles to accept God's will. Because it's Passover, he must remain within the city limits of Jerusalem, and this puts him within reach of his enemies. An armed crowd led by Judas, who knows right where to find Jesus among the mass of pilgrims, seizes him and brings him before the Sanhedrin for questioning. The other disciples flee but Peter, true to his word, stays as close to Jesus as he can. But when he's recognized, he must choose between identifying with Jesus or denying him in order to escape.

READING

Read these next episodes in Act VI out loud like a play, beginning with "They went to a place called Gethsemane" and ending with "And he broke down and wept." Have people take these parts:

- Narrator

- Jesus
- Judas
- False witnesses
- High priest
- Servant girl
- Peter
- Bystanders

DISCUSSION

1 Jesus knows what sufferings are coming and he doesn't want to go through them—no one would. At the same time, he does want to fulfill God's will, which is for him to give his life as a ransom for many. This inner conflict makes him "deeply distressed and troubled." He goes with his disciples to a quiet place where he can meet God in prayer. Over a period of several hours he reaches the assurance that all things are under God's control and he definitively affirms his intention to do God's will, whatever the cost.

Jesus tells all of his disciples that he'll be praying, and he specifically asks Peter, James and John to watch and pray with him, but they fall asleep. Jesus warns Peter in particular that without the spiritual strength that comes from prayer, he won't be able to keep his promise never to abandon him. "The spirit is willing, but the flesh is weak." Peter's fears will overcome his best intentions unless like Jesus he draws close to God and gets a renewed sense of his love, power and presence.

> ◌ Have you ever felt that God wanted you to do something that you were very reluctant to do? How did this affect you emotionally and physically? If you're in a situation like this right now, what encouragement or guidance can you get from the experience Jesus has in this episode?

> ◌ Do you think Peter would still have denied Jesus if he'd prayed at Gethsemane instead of sleeping? Why or why not?

2 The other gospel writers say it was Peter who struck the high priest's servant (probably the leader of this armed crowd) with his sword. But Mark describes this assailant simply as "one of those standing near." He similarly leaves anonymous the young man who was "following Jesus" but who fled naked when seized by his garment. Many interpreters speculate that this young man was Mark himself and that he included this striking incident to show he'd witnessed at least some of the events related in his gospel. While this is possible, it can't be established conclusively. Within the narrative, the actions of the two unnamed figures illustrate that beyond the inner circle of disciples, many others also supported Jesus, but ultimately they couldn't resist the armed crowd and abandoned him themselves. One of them is so eager to get away he even leaves his clothes behind!

Peter, by contrast, shows great courage at first. He stays with Jesus, following him right into the inner courtyard of the house where he's being examined. When a servant girl recognizes him in the firelight, he gives an elusive answer ("I don't know what you're talking about") and moves to the passageway between the courtyard and the street, where it's darker and he can escape more easily. But the servant girl tells the bystanders about him, and they're eventually convinced he must be one of Jesus' followers. Threatened and surrounded, Peter denies even knowing Jesus. The rooster crows and he realizes bitterly that he's failed his friend, just as he predicted.

> ◌ Peter denies Jesus, but only after trying to stay with him and watch out for him. The other disciples don't deny Jesus openly, but they slip off quietly into the darkness at Gethsemane. Which is better? Rank the following characters from best to worst, based on the extent to which you think they did right by Jesus: the other disciples, Peter, James, John, Judas, the armed crowd, whoever swung the sword, the young man, the Sanhedrin, the witnesses, the high priest, the servant girl, the bystanders.

> ◌ Think of someone who dared and achieved great things for God but then failed publicly like Peter. Would it have been better if this person had never done for God the things that made their fall so spectacular? Explain.

3 The members of the Sanhedrin think they're dealing with an insurrectionist. They've considered Jesus dangerous all along, and now he's said something that confirms their suspicions: Anyone who would claim that the temple was going to be destroyed must be trying to incite a rebellion against the established order. The problem is, they can't get two witnesses to agree on what he actually said. And Jesus himself isn't helping.

So the high priest tries another approach. He asks Jesus whether he's the Messiah, the Son of God. (He says "Blessed One" to avoid speaking God's name.) This is precisely the question that has run all the way through the gospel of Mark. Jesus finally answers this question with a definitive yes by combining two Scripture passages that have figured prominently in the book. The first is the quotation from Psalm 110 that he asked the crowds about in the temple, which describes the Messiah sitting at God's right hand. The second passage is Daniel's vision of the Son of Man coming with the clouds of heaven. Jesus has repeatedly applied this title to himself and he cited this passage prominently in his prediction of the temple's destruction. In one climactic moment, major thematic threads of the gospel are drawn together as Jesus finally reveals his identity in public to the leaders of the nation. But in response, they call him a blasphemer and decide he deserves to die.

➲ Why do you think the Jewish leaders of Jesus' time didn't understand or believe who he was?

SESSION 23

JESUS GIVES HIS LIFE AS THE SAVIOR OF THE WORLD

Gospel of Mark > Part Two > Act VI: Jesus' Sufferings, Death, and Resurrection, continued

INTRODUCTION

As he was traveling to Jerusalem with his disciples, Jesus warned three times that he'd be rejected by the nation's leaders and put to death. This ominous prediction is now fulfilled as the Sanhedrin bring Jesus to the Roman governor Pilate and demands his execution. Even though Pilate can't see what crime Jesus has committed, under pressure from the crowds he agrees to have him crucified. Jesus is led away to suffer one of the most painful forms of execution ever invented.

Mark is very mindful of his Roman audience as he relates these scenes. The various means he's used to accommodate them throughout the gospel are particularly clustered here. He translates Aramaic words and phrases into Greek so his readers can understand them. He also employs some Latin terms and expressions. He mentions the connection between one of the characters in the story and two people his audience knows. And above all, Mark presents a centurion who witnesses the crucifixion as a model of the kind of faith in Jesus a Roman person can have. He wants his listeners to see themselves in the story and respond to Jesus the same way.

READING

Read the accounts of Jesus' trial before Pilate and his death on the cross out loud like a play, beginning with "Very early in the morning, the chief priests . . . made their plans" and ending with "when the centurion, who stood there in front of Jesus, saw how he died, he said, 'Surely this man was the Son of God!'" Have people take these parts:
- Narrator
- Pilate
- Jesus
- The crowd (the whole group should speak this part together)
- Bystanders at the cross
- Chief priests and teachers of the law
- Centurion

DISCUSSION

1 Pilate interprets the charges against Jesus in light of a violent uprising that has recently taken place in Jerusalem. (He's still holding several leaders of this uprising in prison, awaiting execution.) When Pilate asks Jesus if he's the king of the Jews, he replies in a way that means "there is some truth in what you say." Jesus has never specifically called himself a king, but in response to the high priest's question, he has described his own heavenly enthronement. Still, Jesus is not the leader of an anti-Roman uprising, which is what Pilate means by his question. He's a king, but not that kind of king. The governor himself notes that Jesus hasn't committed any crime in furtherance of this supposed insurrection such as murder, assassination, sabotage, etc. Nevertheless, rather than antagonize the agitated crowds, Pilate condemns Jesus to death as if he really were guilty. He releases Barabbas, who was arrested in the recent uprising, and sends Jesus to the cross with two of the remaining captured rebels.

➲ In what places today is the community of Jesus' followers considered a subversive group that needs to be suppressed? Describe situations you've heard about or relate some of your own experiences. Is there some truth to the idea that Jesus is a real threat to established authorities in this world?

2 The people who mock Jesus are actually speaking the truth about him without realizing it.

The soldiers don't recognize that by falling on their knees and worshipping Jesus as the king of the Jews, they're anticipating what countless other Gentiles like themselves will do sincerely in the years ahead. They are, in fact, the first to crown him as king, even though they do this with thorns.

The people passing by the cross don't recognize that by calling Jesus the one who was going to destroy and rebuild the temple, they've identified a key aspect of his mission. (Indeed, the Jerusalem temple is effectively put out of business when the curtain that sets it apart as sacred space is torn in two from top to bottom. The new temple will now be the multinational community of Jesus' followers.)

The chief priests and teachers of the law don't understand how true their own words are: "He saved others, but he can't save himself!" It's only by sacrificing his own life that Jesus can become the Savior of the world.

This is a final ironic twist on the way Jesus' identity has remained a secret throughout so much of Mark's gospel. The secret is out, but unless a person has eyes to see and ears to hear, they can't understand who Jesus really is—even if they're proclaiming this with their own mouths.

➲ Do you know anyone (including yourself) who once mocked Jesus but who has since put their faith in him? If so, tell their story.

3 Crucifixion was invented by the Persians and developed by the Romans as an excruciatingly painful way of torturing someone to death. The Romans usually used it only for slaves and rebels. A person nailed to a cross would slowly suffocate as their arms and legs became increasingly unable to lift their body so their lungs could fill. Sometimes their agony would last for days. The soldiers increase Jesus' sufferings by beating and torturing him ahead of time.

Jesus knew this fate awaited him when he first started for Jerusalem and told would-be disciples that they needed to take up their own crosses and follow him. Now as the grisly execution begins Jesus refuses a drink (wine mixed with myrrh) that would deaden some of the pain. In Gethsemane he accepted his Father's will, and that's the "cup" he will drink fully here.

Throughout his time on the cross Jesus is ridiculed by the soldiers, the Jewish leaders and the people passing by. Yet he never says a harsh word in response. He speaks only to God in prayer. Darkness covers the land at midday, and when Jesus dies, it's not with a feeble gasp like most victims of crucifixion, but with a strong, loud cry. The Roman centurion commanding the execution squad is so struck by the way Jesus dies on the cross that he exclaims, "Surely this man was the Son of God!" He has probably overseen many crucifixions, but he's never seen anyone go through the experience like this.

⮕ Would you like to have been present to witness Jesus' crucifixion in person? Why or why not?

⮕ What aspects of the way Jesus died are most meaningful to you? What are some of your favorite songs or hymns that describe Jesus' death on the cross? If you wish, sing some of these together at the end of this session.

⮕ If you've never before put your faith in Jesus as your Savior, but you now understand what his death did for you and you'd like to become one of his followers, tell your group about this and ask them to pray with you as you make this commitment.

SESSION 24

JESUS IS BURIED AND RISES FROM THE DEAD

Gospel of Mark > Part Two > Act VI: Jesus' Sufferings, Death, and Resurrection, concluded

INTRODUCTION

Everything Jesus predicted has now happened except for one thing. Each time he foretold his sufferings and death, he also said that after three days he would rise again. The way time is reckoned in this culture, today is the first day, tomorrow is the second day, and the day after tomorrow is the third day. Jesus has been crucified on a Friday, so if his followers remember and believe this saying, they should expect him to rise from the dead on Sunday. They don't, and so they're so stunned and amazed when they find his tomb empty. They hardly know how to respond, and their bewilderment extends to the present day in the confusion over how Mark actually intended his gospel to end. As we conclude our reading and discussion of the book in this session, we'll consider what Mark most likely had in mind.

READING

Have someone read the account of Jesus' burial, beginning with "Some women were watching from a distance" and ending with "Mary Magdalene and Mary the mother of Joseph saw where he was laid."

Next, have someone read the story of Jesus' resurrection, beginning with "When the Sabbath was over" and ending with "They said nothing to anyone, because they were afraid."

Finally, have someone read the longer ending of Mark, beginning with "When Jesus rose early on the first day of the week" and ending with "the Lord worked with them and confirmed his word by the signs that accompanied it." (This passage is in italics in *The Books of the Bible*, and it's in brackets or italics in most other contemporary versions of the Bible.)

DISCUSSION

1 Throughout the gospel of Mark we've had hints that the circle of Jesus' close followers includes women. In session 5, for example, we saw Jesus describe this group as his brothers *and sisters*. In session 21 we saw an unnamed female friend in Bethany pour perfume on Jesus' head to express her devotion. But now we learn the names of three specific women—Mary Magdalene, Mary and Salome—who traveled with Jesus in Galilee to care for his needs. The twelve disciples have now fled, but these women, along with others who've come to Jerusalem with them, stay with Jesus and mournfully observe his crucifixion from a distance. After his death they note where he's buried so they can return after the Sabbath to anoint his body with spices.

One man, Joseph of Arimathea, boldly asks Pilate if he can give Jesus a decent burial—something not always accorded to a crucified criminal. Even though Joseph is a member of the Sanhedrin, he's willing to defy popular feeling and the rest of the Council's wishes to identify with Jesus by treating his body with honor and respect.

> ◗ Because Mary Magdalene served Jesus in Galilee and remained publicly loyal to him in Jerusalem, and especially because she was later instrumental in spreading the news of Jesus' resurrection, she's among the people who are venerated by Eastern Orthodox and Eastern Rite Catholic churches as "Equal to the Apostles." How do you feel about her having this title?

⊃ Mark's description of Joseph of Arimathea as "waiting for the kingdom of God" suggests that he was a sympathizer who wasn't yet openly following Jesus. But the thought that Jesus' body would be left unburied or tossed in a common grave moved him to take a bold public stand. What can be done to help people today who are similarly sympathetic to Jesus recognize the importance of openly becoming his followers?

2 The account of Mary Magdalene, Mary and Salome discovering that Jesus' tomb is empty ends in a way that most readers find unsatisfying. Not only has the great rock been unaccountably moved away from the tomb entrance, and Jesus' body is nowhere to be found, the women also meet a "young man" who seems very much like an angel and who announces that Jesus has risen from the dead. Even though all of this must be stunning and confusing, and even though Jesus' followers must still be afraid of further reprisals, it's hard to believe that the women would say nothing about these remarkable events to anyone. But this is how Mark's gospel ends, at least in the form it was passed on to later generations. (Experts on the text of the Bible are almost universally agreed on this point.) However, this was considered so unsatisfactory that more material was eventually added to give the gospel a "better" ending.

Interpreters have offered different explanations for the original ending of Mark. Some have argued that he stops the story at this point because he wants his Roman audience to be shocked at the thought of what would have happened if the women really had told no one. Of course they eventually did share the news of Jesus' resurrection, once their amazement and fear wore off, because if they hadn't, faith in Jesus would never have reached Rome. The audience is meant to recognize that no matter how dangerous their own present circumstances, they must continue to tell others about Jesus as well. The themes of faith and fear, which Mark has developed throughout his gospel, reach their climax in this ending.

Other interpreters, however, believe that Mark did write more, but it was lost, or that he intended to write more, but never got the chance. They note that Jesus tells his disciples at the Last Supper that after he has risen he will go ahead of them into Galilee. The angel at the tomb tells the women the same thing. Mark shows how every other prediction Jesus makes in the gospel was fulfilled, and these interpreters argue that it's likely he wrote, or intended to write, a final scene in which Jesus meets the disciples in Galilee. Why this scene never made it into the version of Mark that went into circulation is impossible to determine.

> ➲ Think of a book or a story you've read or a movie or television program you've seen that had an ending that didn't really feel like an ending. What effect did this have on you?

> ➲ If you could, would you give Mark a different ending than the one the gospel apparently went into circulation with? Why or why not?

3 Experts on the text of the Bible agree that the longer ending of Mark is not original. (It's missing from the most reliable early manuscripts.) They believe it was instead put together from other accounts of Jesus' resurrection appearances, including those in the other gospels, and added to Mark's work a generation or two after he wrote. Some communities of Jesus' followers consider this longer ending to be Scripture, based on their understanding of that term, while others consider it a valuable piece of tradition that helps us appreciate how Jesus' earliest followers understood the meaning of his resurrection, his ongoing activity on their behalf and their own responsibilities and privileges as believers.

> ➲ In the longer ending of Mark Jesus makes specific promises to protect and empower his followers. Reread this ending and identify what all these promises are. Can we count on them today even if this material wasn't written by Mark?

> ➲ If someone had asked you "Who is Jesus?" before you read and discussed the gospel of Mark, how would you have answered? Would you say anything different now? If so, what parts of Mark helped you see Jesus in new ways?